Rave Reviews for:

The Executive Persuader: How To Be A Powerful Speaker

by Lynda R. Paulson with Tom Watson

"As a keynote speaker for over 20 years, I thought I knew about speaking. I was wrong! *The Executive Persuader* can teach old dogs new tricks. It's a must read for anyone—at any level of experience."

—Dr. Tony Alessandra,
Author of *Non-Manipulative Selling* and *People Smart*

"I greatly enjoyed *The Executive Persuader*. It's a good 'how-to' book with practical solutions to improve virtually every speaker and to lend confidence to the first-timer. As one who frequently gives speeches, I picked up helpful tips and ideas."

—Dianne Feinstein,
Former Mayor of San Francisco

"I wish I'd had it years ago! *The Executive Persuader* is practical and comprehensive. It brings the speech presentation field up to the reality of the '90s."

—Stephen R. Covey,
Author of *The 7 Habits of Highly Effective People*

"Everyone has the ability to speak in front of an audience; most people just don't know they have the ability. This book gives you the confidence to test your natural ability and improve upon it to become a star speaker!"

—Mary Kay Ash,
Chairman Emeritus, Mary Kay Cosmetics, Inc.

"Mandatory reading for anyone who communicates for a living. I refer to *The Executive Persuader* on a regular basis."

—Jim Comiskey,
Author of *How to Start, Expand and Sell A Business*

"Terrific! A fun, interesting and truthful message of how people relate to public speaking. *The Executive Persuader* provides the tools necessary to overcome the jitters and become the dynamic public speaker hidden in each of us."

—William Dart,
Vice-President, Government Affairs,
Illinois Manufacturers' Association

"Lynda Paulson's book makes public speaking easy on my nerves. It's a speech insurance policy . . . a speaker's bible. And, it makes me look good."

—Sally Jordan,
Co-owner, Jordan Winery

"This book helps me actually look forward to the next speaking opportunity. It gives strength to the weak-kneed speaker by inspiring confidence . . . Her techniques work!"

—William C. Finlayson,
President, O'Connor Hospital

"I do a lot of speaking around the country, to audiences ranging from business groups to congressional subcommittees. After reading *The Executive Persuader*, I find that my new preparation and rehearsal techniques have resulted in a definite increase in confidence. Paulson's coaching and her book helped me tremendously to turn my nervous energy into something positive."

—Gerry Kenny,
President, Kenny Construction Company

"For me, facing the media can be a killer. Her advice works!"

—Jack Cakebread,
Owner, Cakebread Winery

"Paulson's book has changed my whole perspective about speaking. I'm much more confident now and my results with audiences are nothing short of phenomenal. Every executive should read this book."

—Ted Santon,
CEO, Lincoln Financial and Insurance Services

"Lynda Paulson's coaching is a must-do for all of our top people. And, her book is an invaluable backup."

—David Stare,
Owner, Dry Creek Winery

"Thanks to your book, I have found myself really enjoying public speaking. It's a great tool to guide presenters through the communication process and has given me a great deal more confidence in my presentations."

—Marc Jones,
Director of Operations, Sutter Surgery Centers Corporation.

"Your book has remained solidly with me in my public speaking. I use it to great advantage."

—J. Douglas Johnson,
President and CEO, G.S. Blodgett Corporation

"For professionals and executives, *The Executive Persuader* combines "beyond-the-basics" substantive knowledge with a user-friendly style."

—Anne Hamblin Schiave,
Attorney, McBride, Baker & Coles

"The book improved my small group communication skills and I found it of great value in becoming a better public speaker."

—Allan Farwell,
General Manager, Park Hyatt Chicago

"In *The Executive Persuader*, you "motivationally educate" professionals to understand and implement realistic tools that have long-lasting applications."

—Nancy J. Stoltenberg,
Corporate Director of Marketing,
Marathon Shopping Center Group

"*The Executive Persuader* is a powerful tool, motivating me to perform at my highest level."

—Richard A. Benson,
Architect

THE EXECUTIVE PERSUADER
How To Be A Powerful Speaker

BY LYNDA R. PAULSON
WITH TOM WATSON

SSI Publishing
Napa, California

The Executive Persuader:
How to Be a Powerful Speaker

Copyright © 1991 SSI Publishing
1325 Imola Ave. West, Suite 404
Napa, California 94559

Library of Congress Cataloging-in-Publication Data

Paulson, Lynda R., with Tom Watson.
 The Executive Persuader: How to Be a Powerful Speaker

 1. Public Speaking. 2. Business Communication. 3. Executive Training.
 4 Career Advancement. 5. Media Appearances.
 I. Watson, Tom. II. Title

 Bibliography: p. 165
 Index: p. 167
 p. cm.
 PN4121   808.5'1   90-63563

                                        QB190-84
                                          MARC
 ISBN 0-9628039-6-0

Cover Design by Robert Howard, Fort Collins, CO
Book Production by Comp-Type, Inc., Fort Bragg, CA
Publicity and Sales by Lagoon Publications, Napa, CA
Printed in the United States of America

Dedication

To the treasured memory of Tom Watson, without whose wit, warmth and extraordinary skill this book would still be in my mind. Tom helped many people see into their own hearts and find their talents. And, he made me laugh.

CONTENTS

The Executive Persuader: How To Be A Powerful Speaker is available at special quantity discounts for bulk purchases by businesses and associations for sales promotions, premiums, fund raising or educational use. Book excerpts can also be made available for publication.

For details, contact Karen Misuraca
                     Lagoon Publications
                     783 Magellan Way
                     Napa, CA 94559
                     Phone/Fax (707) 226-9410.

INTRODUCTION

"Who is that guy?" the vice president of Conoco Oil Company wanted to know. He was seated to my right on the podium and had leaned around behind me to ask the vice president of sales, who was seated on my left.

"John Smith . . . our sales office, why?" came the quick response. It was a normal, routine business meeting for a division of the large company. I was there to make a presentation but, before I was introduced, a company official had given out some information and had asked for feedback. The young man had stood, made a couple of rather astute comments and asked a penetrating question.

"He should be in our management program," replied the senior executive. And, the way he said it, even an eavesdropper could tell it was going to happen.

Wham! This eager young person's career had taken a quantum leap. The whole process couldn't have lasted more than 45 seconds.

Luck? Natural charisma? A rare occurrence? Don't you believe it. As a communications coach and consultant, I could have predicted it would happen sooner or later.

Why? That young man had personal presence. He exuded confidence, he showed he could think on his feet and he had developed the skills to articulate his ideas quickly and with power.

I see it happen all the time and you probably do, too.

- A new president steps into a struggling, near bankrupt company, and huddles briefly with its key players. In a matter of days even skeptical creditors and badly dispirited employees are beginning to believe the executive is going to somehow turn the company around.

- A middle manager, an engineer or a supervisor comes out of nowhere, makes an impressive presentation and is suddenly catapulted into a key executive slot.

- A salesperson, after working for weeks, finally gets the ear of a top decision maker for 20 minutes and walks out with a major order.

- A professional person (doctor, lawyer, psychologist) starts making a big impact in television interviews and as a featured speaker at conferences. Almost overnight, the professional's name becomes a respected household word, without a dollar being spent on advertising or promotion.

The message is simple: People who can get their ideas across quickly, clearly and with power, seem to get things done and stay a step ahead in the business or professional realm.

That fact is confirmed by every major survey of top managers of Fortune 500 companies. They consistently rate an ability to communicate as the most crucial ingredient for career growth; above technical knowledge and expertise, above management and political savvy, even above experience.

The ability to communicate is *the* leadership ability, the one that energizes all others.

Owning the skill to communicate your ideas and passions can open doors for you and your organization like nothing else can, whatever your position, your function or your objectives.

I'd bet that what I just told you didn't come as a big surprise. In the '80s, the U.S. went through eight years of watching an administration survive scandal after scandal, a record-setting budget deficit, an unprecedented trade imbalance and constant attacks by hostile media and political opponents. Yet President Ronald Reagan not only survived, he emerged from office as one of the most popular presidents of this century because he had a well-deserved reputation as "the great communicator." He had the ability to make people believe him, respond positively to him and do what he asked them to do. That's what it means to have personal presence, poise and power.

The Other Side Of The Coin

Unfortunately, few business and professional people are effective communicators. Maybe that's why it's those few who make such an impact.

- How many people can hold an audience spellbound and get their listeners to do precisely what they want done?

- How many times have you seen a real expert in some field—someone you knew was very knowledgeable and capable—freeze up in front of a group or give an ineffective, forgettable presentation?

- How many times have you seen business or professional leaders squirm their way through media interviews and make already bad public perceptions even worse?

- How many good ideas, proposals and plans have you seen sabotaged by boring, disjointed or ineffective presentations?

- How many capable and promising people have you seen permanently sidelined because their superiors felt they didn't have the personal presence and communications skills needed to carry a higher position?

You've probably seen all of these examples of people being held back by their inability to grab the attention of others and motivate them.

Why Aren't People Better Communicators?

We all know that our ability to get people to respond positively to us can make or break us in the business and professional world. It can even have a big impact on our personal and social lives. Why don't more people do something about it?

Certainly, lack of motivation and desire is a big factor. I won't address that reason, because if you lacked desire, you wouldn't have picked up this book. Besides, this book is not about "shoulds" and "oughts," it's about "whys" and "hows."

During my career as a communications coach, instructor and consultant, I've discovered four big reasons why people don't get better.

(1) *Most people think they are better speakers and communicators than they are, so they don't make improvement a priority.*

One of the first things we do in our Executive Speaking Experience seminars is to videotape each participant and critique their presentation. The camera is brutally frank. It doggedly follows the facial expressions and gestures, it relentlessly tracks the eyes and it mercilessly exposes any personal discomfort or lack of confidence.

Oddly enough, it's a great exercise for building rapport at the seminar.

Suddenly, CEOs from big companies, highly respected professionals and people from all walks of life have several things in common:

A) They are all on equal footing and the only thing that matters is their ability to communicate with their new-found peers;

B) They've discovered their flaws in a non-threatening environment;

C) They feel supportive of and supported by each other.

Once people see how they really come across to others, becoming better communicators very quickly becomes a pressing priority. Even those who are sent by their companies, and come a little reluctantly, get quite involved in the process.

Try it sometime. Give a short presentation in front of a studio-grade video camera, and have a skilled professional critique you. But make sure you get someone who has the skills to do it right and the tact to do it gently. Otherwise, it can be devastating.

(2) *People often don't get better at communicating because they think it's harder than it is and takes much longer than it does.*

Speaking and communicating are arts in which anyone can improve, no matter how long they've been at it or how good they are. I've been speaking professionally, in one form or another, for over a decade and I still learn something from every seminar and coaching experience.

You can achieve dramatic improvements quickly and easily, by studying this book, by practicing and by getting feedback. Our seminar participants look back at their first videos after only five days and can't believe how far they've come.

(3) *Other people don't become good speakers and communicators because they think it requires some in-born talent or natural charisma they don't have.*

Natural talent helps. If you think of Winston Churchill, or John F. Kennedy or Eleanor Roosevelt, you know they had something special.

But, if you look a little deeper, you'll discover that the "something special" came more from passion and hard work than from genetics.

All of us have what it takes to be effective communicators if we're willing to pay the price and get the right guidance.

(4) *Many people, some who work very hard at it, don't get better at communicating because they're being steered in the wrong direction.*

Everywhere there are books, cassette albums, newsletters, courses and coaches trying to teach people how to speak effectively. With a few notable exceptions, most of them create more problems for would-be speakers than they solve.

The biggest problem is that most teachers and coaches major on minors. You can find hundreds of sources that tell you how to stand, how to hold a microphone and how to put together a good speech. But those are mechanical, common sense concerns that play only a small part in the total picture.

The real issues of public speaking are: how to grab an audience by the heart as well as the head, how to build personal credibility and presence, how to "feel" an audience and make them "feel" you, how to make people care and understand and do what you want them to do.

Speaking: The Strategic Dimension

All speaking (except self-talk) is public speaking, whether you're speaking to one person or an audience of thousands. It's also true whether you're talking on a telephone, participating in a tele-conference or speaking to millions through the media.

In fact, you cannot *not* communicate! After every verbal or nonverbal message exchange, your personal stock either goes up or comes down, usually in direct ratio to how well you speak and present yourself.

What's more, speaking is a results-producing business or professional function. Ultimately, every word you speak or imply impacts upon both the sales and profits of any organization you represent and on your own career growth.

If you understand those facts, and know what to do with them, speaking can give you a tremendous strategic advantage in any arena where you compete. Effective speaking is vital to your leadership task of communicating vision, mission and goals.

But let me get very personal with you about speaking. Do you ever feel a burning passion you can't quite seem to ignite in others? Ever have an idea you somehow can't articulate? Ever feel intimidated by audiences or video and sound equipment? Ever bungle or walk away from opportunities because you're not quite up to the challenge? Ever wish you could do a better job of motivating, leading or impressing people?

If you answered "yes" to any of those questions, you're going to love this book.

What You Can Expect From This Book

Many books offer tips on how to speak, but few really focus on how to get the most mileage out of your speaking experience. *The Executive Persuader* teaches you strategies and tactics, not gimmicks and tricks.

Certainly, you'll pick up plenty of practical pointers and useful techniques. More than that, however, you'll learn how to make people sit up and pay attention to you, how to discover and take advantage of your strongest personal selling points and how to come across like a pro in any setting.

The kinds of people I work with day in and day out are not college professors who want to learn theories, or amateurs who dream of being able to give a good talk to their garden club, or speakers who want to pick up new gimmicks or jokes.

These corporate chairmen, CEOs, executives, managers and professionals see speaking as a tool for getting things done. Some are salespeople and leaders who need to become more articulate and persuasive.

They're being promoted into positions where they need to prove how much savvy they have.

These are the kinds of issues I'll focus on in this book. My primary emphasis will be on speaking to groups, the kinds of groups you'd expect to encounter in your business or professional setting.

Of course, learning how to speak to groups has a very useful side benefit. Everything you learn about speaking in front of groups can be adapted to working with people in one-to-one situations. For instance, when you learn how to be more poised in front of a large group, you can apply the same principles to meeting with your boss, your staff, your clients or even to social settings. Discovering how to project more of your personal presence through a microphone, you can speak more powerfully on the telephone, on videotapes and on TV.

So, if becoming a more powerful communicator is what you want, let's make a deal up front. I'll promise not to tell you anything I have not tested and proven effective with my clients if you'll agree not dismiss any idea without at least giving it a try. Agreed?

Now, let's get started.

CHAPTER ONE

THE POWER OF PERSONAL POSITIONING

"You are the message."
—*Roger Ailes*

I magine this tough assignment—you're appearing before a U.S. Senate appropriations subcommittee, representing a group that is asking for an allocation of $2.4 billion, at a time when virtually all requests for additional funding are being axed.

To add to the challenge, the committee is chaired by Senator William Proxmire, the self-appointed watchdog of federal spending and issuer of "The Golden Fleece Awards" for government waste.

You watch as one speaker after another is herded through the procedure, like so many sheep. Each is given about three-and-a-half minutes before the committee, whose members seem more intent on talking to each other and reading the written requests they've been given than in listening to anything a speaker has to say.

One by one, the speakers hurriedly read through the highlights of their budget requests, deliver their prepared remarks, answer a question or two, then find themselves quickly escorted out. Most requests are systematically cut in half, and many are denied entirely.

That's exactly the scenario Gerry Kenny faced in 1988 when he was the designated spokesman for a clean water bill. Besides, he knew that Senator Proxmire had already gone on record as wanting to cut his request by at least 25%, maybe more.

But Gerry was too savvy a presenter to roll over and play dead, which is what everybody else seemed to be doing. As CEO of the Chicago-based Kenny Construction Company, a large firm which builds bridges and tunnels all over America, he'd been around the block a few times.

"I knew two things," Gerry later told a graduating class of my Executive Speaking Experience. "First, I knew I didn't want them to brush me aside like they were doing everybody else and, second, I knew I'd have to do something dramatically different to keep it from happening."

So, in a very conversational and matter-of-fact tone, Gerry began his presentation by almost doubling his request. He asked for $4.2 billion.

Every senator on the panel sat up straight in his chair and stared at Gerry.

"That must be a typo," said Chairman Proxmire, "You're asking for $2.4 billion, not $4.2 billion, aren't you?"

"No" Gerry replied with calm confidence. "We want the full $4.2 billion you promised us four years ago."

While he had their attention, he hit them with several of his strongest arguments. That triggered at least ten minutes of serious questioning from all the committee members. When he was finished, several of the senators followed him out into the hallway to ask further questions.

No, he didn't get the $4.2 billion, but he did get every dollar of the $2.4 billion in his original written request. His strategy worked because it positioned him as a person to be reckoned with, not as someone who could be easily intimidated by either the hearing process or the illustrious senators.

In a later chapter, you'll discover how Gerry Kenny was able to recognize the hazard he faced, why he had the confidence to use his shock treatment to get the attention of the panel and why it worked so effectively.

Personal Positioning Is Managing Perceptions

Most executives and professionals recognize the power of

personal positioning. They believe that what Tom Peters and Bob Waterman say is true, that "perception is reality." So they give a great deal of attention to the way others perceive them.

Many CEO's read books like John T. Molloy's excellent *Dress For Success* and *Live For Success*. Some go so far as to have their clothes custom designed to highlight their best features. Others contract with image consultants to find the colors, styles and accessories that will give them the most impact.

And, when it comes to environments, they go all out with professionally decorated offices, homes and showrooms, they drive the right cars, and they always make sure they are seen at the right places.

Even if we don't go the designer and customization route, most of us try to package ourselves in a way that influences positively the perceptions of others about us and whatever we represent.

Playing The Pro/Am

Unfortunately, too many executives and professionals stop far short in their efforts to position themselves for maximum impact. They either fail to recognize the power of public speaking as a positioning tool and leave the task to their subordinates or professional presenters or, if they do speak, they give little attention to how well they do it and end up coming across like amateurs.

Why is it so crucial for every key player in an organization to speak to groups as often and as effectively as possible?

Because nine out of ten people surveyed say that the human element is the most crucial factor to be managed in any business or profession.

And, what's the most crucial function in managing the human element? Again, nine out of ten people say it's communicating effectively with the human beings who can make or break your dreams and visions, the myriads of stakeholders who own, run, produce for, buy from or make and enforce laws that affect your organization.

Yet, where do most people in management and the professions invest most of their energies? In the technical side, or in finances, or in marketing, or in management theories.

Finally, it has begun to dawn upon the real movers and shakers in business and the professions that communication is *the* critical function, the one which energizes, guides and controls all other functions.

To put it bluntly:

- What you know and can do does not matter nearly so much as what you are able to communicate to other people. And, in the new business and professional arena, that's becoming increasingly true.

- Your success in your chosen marketplace will be directly proportional to your ability to distinguish yourself and your products or services in the minds of your potential customers/clients. The better you can communicate your differential advantage, the more successful you can be.

- Your effectiveness in mobilizing and guiding the people who work for and with you will depend almost totally on your ability to articulate your vision, sell your mission, clarify your strategies and make people care about your goals.

- Your career and professional growth will be shaped by your ability to create and maintain the right perceptions in the minds of the key people who can control your opportunities.

More than any other factor or combination of factors, your personal or corporate success depends upon your ability to influence the way you and your causes are perceived by the people who can help you reach your goals. As a professional, you simply cannot afford to perform like an amateur.

The Audience's Perceptions Of You

Our culture runs on meetings. Sooner or later, you're going to be making presentations of some sort, at least to small groups.

You may be a real pro at what you do, but how good are you at communicating it to other people? How good are you at presenting your expertise, your ideas and your vision?

The sheriff in the movie *Cool Hand Luke* was mistaken when he kept saying "What we've got here is a failure to communicate." You cannot "fail to communicate." Everything you do or say communicates something. The way you look, act, express yourself—everything about you—speaks clearly to those you encounter.

What's communicated might be positive or negative; it may contribute to or detract from the achievement of your goals; it may enhance or diminish your standing with people; but an impression is always formed, a message always comes through.

So, failure to communicate is not an option. You always communicate. As I repeatedly say to my clients "You cannot *not* communicate."

The process goes on around us all day, every day. We can't simply refuse to communicate. Even if we refuse to say anything, that sends a message. If we choose to withdraw from human contact, our absence communicates something about us. We can choose how effectively we will take charge of the messages we send; how well we will manage the communications process.

Audiences Don't Respond To Speeches

Have you ever noticed what happens at a convention or a conference? Some sessions are loaded with people, while at others, you can get pretty lonely, regardless of the topic.

You'll hear, "Let's slip out and do some sightseeing (or get a few beers) this afternoon."

"Who's speaking in that session?" someone will ask.

"Oh, it's just Joe (or Mary) . . . we won't miss much."

"You're right, but I don't want to miss that session tonight . . . . I've heard that speaker is great!"

What makes the difference? Audiences don't respond to speeches, they respond to speakers. They'll forget in a heartbeat what a speaker said, but they will remember for years:

- How the speaker made them feel

- How impressed (positively or negatively) they were

- How solid the speaker's presentation was

- How the speaker came across.

I often ask my clients in private coaching sessions, "What reputation are you building among the audiences you address?"

The same thing goes on in personal contacts. People who can influence your career or cause notice how clearly and concisely you express ideas. They observe whether you get right to the point or ramble all over the place. They sense whether or not you know what you're talking about.

Oh, maybe they don't sit around and analyze your speaking style and habits, or the kinds of gestures you make. But, they're aware of how they experience you—as powerful, astute, clear and persuasive, or as muddled, confusing and lacking in credibility.

"You Are The Message"

Roger Ailes is right, you know. You really are the message. People respond to speakers, not to speeches.

Ever since John Alden tried to convey the affection of Captain Miles Standish to the lovely Priscilla Mullins, and she asked "Why don't you speak for yourself, John?", we've known that there is tremendous power in personal presence.

Corporations spend upwards of $250 per sales call to keep salespeople in the field because they know there is nothing as persuasive as the personal touch. AT&T has made a fortune by telling people to "Reach out and touch someone." Victor Kiam and Mary Kay Ash have demonstrated how much impact top-flight executives can have when they are willing to go person-to-person with customers, employees, stockholders and the general public.

You will be amazed at what you can accomplish by speaking to groups in person and through the media.

An illustration:

A "wimp" candidate named George Bush, who was "born with a silver foot in his mouth," walks into "an ambush" by the ultimate predator of news anchors, Dan Rather.

It's a setup all the way, from the dwarfing chair the producers give the candidate to the camera angles which make him appear to be looking up at his interrogator; from the lighted global map behind the anchorman to the power suit and tie he wears.

Anchor Rather assumes the posture of prosecutor for the American people. The subject turns to Candidate Bush's involvement in the Iran-Contra affair. The "wimp" backs away from the subject and the prosecutor comes after him, each question becoming more aggressive in tone.

Finally, Bush turns and calls it "an ambush." The subject shifts to the tactics of the anchor and his network. The phone starts ringing off the hook, ten to one in favor of the candidate.

Abruptly, the candidate is cut off in mid-sentence by the show's producer.

A disaster? Not on your life. The polls showed that the "wimp factor" was disproven, that Iran-Contra became a non-issue in the campaign, and soon the candidate was free to talk about a "kinder, gentler America." Within weeks, Rather is forced to call him President-elect Bush.

George Bush demonstrated through that encounter the awesome power of personal positioning. People who know how to handle themselves in person and on the media can achieve almost unbelievable results.

The Coin Of The New Realm

As we dash headlong toward the mystical year 2000, a new power base is emerging, and we're just beginning to understand the dynamics of Marshall McLuhan's view of the world as a "global village."

John Naisbitt, Alvin Toffler and other futurists are calling this "the information age." They're saying that information will be the power base of the future, like raw materials, capital and equipment were the coin of the realm in the past.

Think about what that means. It's not that information is power. Information is like money; it's not how much you have but how you use it that determines the good it will do.

We're being bombarded with information. There's so much data, in fact, that most people can't comprehend and deal with it. So, those people who can sort through all the raw data, translate it into useful information and present it in clear and meaningful ways will increasingly become the power brokers.

That's the good news. The bad news is that those who can't handle themselves well in our increasingly communicative world will be bypassed.

Among professionals, self-promotion has become a way of life. Doctors, lawyers, psychologists and others who long disdained the idea of promoting as unprofessional are facing massive competition from a new breed who see it as a normal part of achieving success.

Meanwhile, as technology is making it easier to communicate intimately with larger numbers of people, a changing work ethic and customer service demands are making it necessary to do so.

Many of my clients who once hid behind closed doors are finding that it pays rich dividends to reach out to people through videotape, closed circuit television hookups and other high tech media. Tele-conferencing is gradually becoming the new way to meet, and soon we'll find ourselves presenting ideas in video-conferences, complete with three-dimensional holographic images.

The Power Of The Presenter

Technology is heightening the demand for capable presenters, not diminishing it, as some had predicted.

But technology and the realities of the new global marketplace are also changing the ground rules for all forms of presentation. Many of the techniques and strategies that were very effective a decade ago no longer work. To be a viable communicator in the information age poses a major challenge to the best presenters.

Let's look at some of the emerging trends in presentations and what they imply for those who would be powerful presenters.

(1) *Compacting:* Television's five-second sound bite and thirty-second interview have attuned the masses to quickie presentations. It hasn't been long since a typical boardroom presentation lasted 30 minutes or more; but those days are gone forever. Now, it's not unusual for a presenter to be allotted three minutes to cover a major topic.

That means the window of attention is so narrow you have to be able to hit fast and hard.

(2) *Personalization:* According to the *Wall Street Journal*, the average American receives more than 5,000 advertising messages a day. Add all the verbal interchanges, telephone calls and written messages we are bombarded with and you can see why it's so hard to get anybody to pay attention to what you have to say. To have any hope of being heard above all the competing voices, your presentations have to be so personalized and so attuned to the priorities of your targeted audience that they cannot be ignored.

(3) *Entertainment:* Many people in our culture are suffering from sensory overload. After all, what can you do to impress people after they've seen laser shows, multi-media presentations and Star Wars gimmickry? When people can ignore the steady stream of mass killings, starvation and disasters that parade through their living rooms each night, how can you get them excited about anything?

Smart speakers are increasingly utilizing humor, stories and metaphors to drive home their points. Perhaps most important of all, we have to be able to touch people where they live—to make them laugh and cry and care very deeply about what we say.

(4) *Targeting:* With computers spewing out data like volcanic lava and data banks connecting people instantaneously with more information than they could process in a lifetime, it's hard to come up with something people have not heard before. It's not at all unusual to face an audience that is suffering from mental fatigue.

That means we have to do our homework, both with our audiences and our presentation. We have to focus vital information. There has to be a uniqueness in what we say and in the way we say it.

(5) *Building Credibility:* Skepticism is widespread these days. People no longer accept ideas and orders simply because they come from the top down or from an "honored" professional. Besides, people have heard so many sales pitches and so much hype that they question everything they hear, and systematically challenge many assumptions that seem self-evident to the speakers.

To counter the skepticism, speakers have to work hard at building credibility. We not only have to make sure that what we say is true, we have to make it convincing and believable.

(6) *Individuation:* The mass media tend to homogenize everything to make it appeal to as many people as possible. Just as business and the professions are finding that con-

sumers want more customization and individual attention in products and services, speakers are finding that audiences are made up of individuals who want to be recognized as persons, not herded together with everyone else.

That's why more and more meetings are running multi-track programs. To have impact in a homogenized world, we have to maintain strong eye contact and, whenever possible, move out into the audience and connect with individual human beings.

(7) *Simplification:* Our world is growing increasingly complex and confusing. High technology, cross-pollenization of cultures and the trend toward bigness make it harder and harder for people to find a place to plug in. What most do is to find little niches which they can comprehend and fit into, and stay with their narrow points of identification.

To have any hope of registering our messages with our audiences, we have to greatly over-simplify them and then repeat them again and again until they begin to sink in.

(8) *Visualization:* Television, movies, video, the print media, billboards and even architecture have so heightened visual stimulation that audiences now get bored very quickly with anything that isn't colorful, doesn't move or doesn't change frequently.

So, speakers are learning to make the most of their gestures and expressions. They're also using more lively visual aids and appealing to all of our senses. To break through to our audiences, we have to make each speech a total experience.

(9) *Feedback:* Some of the by-products of all the complexity and rapid change are confusion, misunderstandings and false perceptions. People often don't hear what we say, or understand what we mean or apply it in the way we want them to.

Wise speakers know that all effective communication is dialog. Thus, they try to get their audiences involved and make them active participants in the on-going dialog.

(10) *Reinforcement:* Studies have shown that half of what a speaker says is forgotten within an hour after it's been said. Within 24 hours, nearly 90% of the content of a speech is forgotten by audience members.

We simply have to give people handles they can use to hang onto the important points we make. Such tools as symbolism, visual reinforcement and repetition are becoming increasingly important.

If all this sounds like gaining and holding the attention of an audience in today's media-saturated world is a tough challenge, you have read correctly. And, as they say in the movies, "You ain't seen nothing yet!"

Give It Your Best Shot

Learning how to come across as powerful and effective in front of a group is simple. But just because something is simple doesn't mean it's easy. It's simple to run a marathon—all you have to do is keep picking them up and putting them down. But anybody who has tried it will quickly tell you it's not easy.

Yet, think about it: If you are the message, and if so much is riding on your ability to position yourself through speaking, why not approach it with the same tenacity and creative energy you apply to every other critical function of your profession?

If you're already good, you can become better, maybe even superb. If you don't feel really comfortable and competent at it, you can conquer those feelings and become a relaxed, capable speaker by mastering a few basics.

The rewards are incredible. Believe me, I've worked with hundreds of executives, professionals, politicians and other people, and I've seen what happens when they start getting great responses from their audiences. Many of them can't believe they could be so relaxed, so confident, or so effective.

Now, I'm going to show you a dynamite way you can boost your ratings with every audience.

CHAPTER TWO

YOU ARE YOUR POWER

"When you hear him, you button your coat
to keep from taking a cold."
—*Critic of 19th century orator Edward Everett*

Roger B. Smith has discovered how crucial communicating with audiences can be in running a corporation, and how tough it can be to get through to them.

As board chairman of General Motors during one of the giant automaker's most turbulent decades, the 1980s, Smith found himself defending one controversial decision after another.

- The $48-billion drive he spearheaded to automate GM's factories was constantly challenged by the United Auto Workers as a ploy to weaken the union's influence and by the financial community as spending too much too fast.

- When the high-tech equipment went on-line, it didn't work properly. The robots broke too many parts and computer software glitches often slowed production to a crawl.

- Quality, sales, profits and market share dropped perilously. Some 40,000 workers were laid off and most of the 750,000 others were confused by management shifts, reorganizations and policy changes. Morale plunged.

- Meanwhile, rivals Ford, Chrysler and the foreign car makers were scoring big gains. Even manufacturers from third world countries like South Korea were chipping away at the domain GM had dominated so long.

- To add to the confusion, Smith was besieged by billionaire H. Ross Perot and corporate lawyer Elmer W. Johnson, who fought vigorously for sweeping changes, including the ouster of Smith as chairman.

Eventually, the veteran executive decided to take his and GM's case to the people. He began speaking frequently to groups of corporate managers, employees, stockholders and even in public forums and through the media.

One of his toughest challenges in breaking through to those audiences was dispelling his image as cold, aloof, insensitive and uncaring. People closest to him knew the image to be a bum rap and counseled him to let his real personality come out by being more spontaneous in his speeches and responses to criticisms.

Gradually, a new Roger Smith began to emerge. A *Wall Street Journal* article highlighted the metamorphosis with a story which symbolized the new style:

A. Hansen, a mid-level executive, stood up to report from Table 37. "We would really appreciate it if you could lick the temperature problem in this corner of the room," he complained.

Chairman Roger B. Smith's typically imperious response: "I've got a sweater on. One of the things we've got to do in this corporation is find 15-cent solutions to million-dollar problems."

Undeterred, Mr. Hansen shot back: "Could I please borrow your sweater?"

The crowd laughed nervously, but Mr. Smith calmly climbed off the stage, walked to the back of the room, took off his brown cardigan and handed it to Mr. Hansen. He then strode back to the podium amid enthusiastic applause.

From that moment on, Chairman Smith had the group of executives eating out of his hand. He demonstrated that the best way for any speaker to get response, no matter who he or she is, is to get real.

Why Do Most Speeches Fizzle?

Let's face it: most speeches are duds, especially those made by people who are experts at something but amateurs at speaking.

Usually, meeting planners drum up a crowd with heavy pre-promotion, someone gives a glowing introduction, and we're sitting there thinking: "Wow! this ought to be something special." Then what happens? Most often, we are treated to a speech that has only three things wrong with it:

(1) It's read.

(2) It's read poorly.

(3) It's not worth reading.

The result is a little like a headline the *London Times* ran during the late 1950s when the United States was trying desperately to save face after being upstaged by Russia's shocking launch of Sputnik One. After months of hype and media attention, the eyes of the world were on Cape Canaveral. But NASA's launch attempt fizzled. The taunting *Times* headline read: "10-9-8-7-6-5-4-3-2-1-PFFFT."

Halfway Up A Mountain

Actually, as we saw in chapter one, it's not speeches that fail, it's speakers.

When I say most speakers fail, it's not that they get booed off the stage, or that they get no response at all or even that people walk out shaking their heads and talking about how bad they were. It's just that they blow so many golden opportunities.

Our word "mediocre" comes from two Latin words, "medi" and "ocris," which mean "halfway up a mountain." The primary definition of mediocre is "of low quality: ordinary."

Of course, being halfway up a mountain is okay if that's as

high as you want to go, or even if you give it your best effort and it's all you can do.

But it's not unusual to see top notch executives and professionals give mediocre presentations, when they would chew out a subordinate in a New York minute for doing no better in almost any other area of business.

From Dud To Dynamite

If you've spoken, even to small groups, you know what I'm talking about. You either connect with the audience or you don't.

When you don't connect, the response is just not there. The laughter is courteous, the feedback restrained, and the applause quickly fades into the noise of opening exit doors. If you've got an ounce of pride or competitiveness in you, you'd rather crawl into a hole than stand and face the forced smiles and shallow compliments of your friends and those who dare not leave without shaking your hand.

But when you connect, really connect, with an audience, it's a whole different experience. They hang onto your every word and pause, their gestures show they're caught up in what you're saying, they can't take their eyes off you, they move with you, even seem to breathe with you. They anticipate your punchlines and their body signals (if they move at all) keep egging you on.

"I think I'm addicted," Sam Thompson shouted when he called me one day after just that kind of encounter with an audience of 400 women. Sam is vice president of a firm in Indianapolis that specializes in marketing lifestyle products.

"Addicted to what? Women?" I teased.

"No, to speaking!" Sam said; then he explained what had happened. "When I walked into that auditorium and saw 400 women sitting there, I panicked! I've never spoken to that many people before; let alone, all women.

"But I kept telling myself I could do it . . . that they were going to love me, just like you told us in the course. Once I got on stage, I could feel my energy and enthusiasm rising," he said.

"Before long, I could feel the energy coming back from them. They laughed, cried, cheered, and, when I'd finished, they wouldn't let me go. They kept asking me questions, long past the time to quit. I never felt so high!" he bubbled on.

Now, here is a person who is very successful in his business and has been on stage as an amateur actor many times over the years.

"Haven't you ever had that kind of response when you were acting?" I asked.

"It's different when you're speaking," he said. "It's like you're giving your mind and heart and soul to them, and they can't get enough of you!"

Well, it's not always that rapturous, but connecting with an audience at a very deep level is one of the most fulfilling and productive experiences you can ever have.

Why Don't More Speakers Connect Like That?

But why don't most speakers get through to their audiences like Sam or Roger Smith did? The biggest reason is that when most speakers stand up in front of a group, they stiffen up and turn into talking heads.

The most competent, forceful, charming and witty professionals often become like zombies when they step onto a stage. Oh, their lips move and they talk (more or less), but their passionate souls and dynamic personalities seem to be held captive in their stick-like bodies.

It's fear. And that's tough to admit to ourselves, much less to anybody else.

Face it: it's frightening to stand there with all eyes focused on you. What if you give them everything you've got and it's not enough? What if you show them the best of your personality and they don't like you? What if you make a fool of yourself or say the wrong thing? What if you feel vulnerable and they take advantage of your weak spots?

It's risky business, this getting up in front of people you care about and laying your self on the line. No wonder people hide behind a lectern and bury their eyes in a script. The maneuver is a little like whistling while you walk by a graveyard on a dark night.

The biggest problem with getting caught up in the talking head and stick body syndrome is that it focuses on how *you* are experiencing the process, not on how *your audience* is experiencing you.

Most inexperienced speakers think that what they have to say is the most important element of giving a speech, but the old pros know that the opposite is true. The power of our personal presence is the greatest thing any of us have going for us.

You Are Your Power

Most people can read and comprehend more content in half-an-hour than you could ever get across in the same time through speaking. Add the time consumed in going to and from a meeting, and a speech is not the most efficient way to get your content across.

We speak, not because it's efficient, but because it's effective. We speak because we want people to experience our convictions, our passions, our excitement. We want what is real to us to become real to others. We want them to understand what we know, to care about what we believe, to do something in response to what they receive.

What makes speaking so powerful is that at least 85% of what we communicate in speaking is non-verbal. It's what people see in our eyes, in our movements and in our actions. It's what they hear through the tone of our voice. It's what they sense on a subliminal level. That's why speaking, to a group or one-on-one, is such a total experience.

It makes sense then, doesn't it, that the greatest hope you have for making people hear and believe and care about what you have to say is to let them experience the full force of your total personhood?

The problem is that most speakers think they're doing that, but few ever really do. And those few are the ones who leave us saying "Wow!"

". . . To See Ourselves As Others See Us."

Robert Burns lamented centuries ago that it would free us from "many a blunder" if we could only "see ourselves as others see us." But that's not easy to do. Try following the movement of your own eyes in a mirror sometime. Make the slightest movement and you lose contact with this most revealing window into the soul. And, it's not very helpful to ask someone else how you come across because their appraisals will be colored by their biases. Besides, most people are amateurs at analyzing the way you come across to an audience.

But, at last, the great Scottish poet's prayers have been answered. The "giftie" of electronics has given us the power to see ourselves as others see us. It's called videotape and it reveals exactly how you come across to other people. It helps you get rid of your liabilities and make the most of your assets.

The Road To Building Personal Presence

"I almost had a stroke when I first saw myself on video," Anne Schiave once told me. Anne is a sharp attorney-at-law with McBride, Baker and Coles in Chicago.

Personal presence is not only an asset to an attorney, it's a matter of survival. Whether you're meeting with a client, or negotiating an agreement through another attorney, or arguing the merits of a case in a judge's chambers, or presenting arguments before a jury, you're always on stage. The one thing you have to be is convincing.

Now, Anne had several things working against her.

First, she is a woman on what is still—despite all the gains women have made recently—predominantly a man's turf.

Second, she's very small; almost petite. You could easily overlook her in a crowded room.

Third, she has a tendency to speak very softly.

Those were her liabilities.

But, does she ever have assets!

To start with, she has enough sincerity in her eyes to melt away the doubts of the most hardened cynic.

Second, her face is very expressive and lively.

Third, her voice, although soft, has a rich quality to it that further enhances her natural warmth and sincerity.

Fourth, while her gestures tend to be subdued, they look real and natural.

Orchestrating Anne

All Anne had to do to create more credibility was to learn how to orchestrate her strengths, how to amplify what she already had going for her and to compensate for her liabilities.

One of the first things she did was to practice making better use of her eyes and facial expressions. She built more trust by maintaining better eye contact, she showed more of her sincerity by accenting her facial expressions and she worked on the way she held her head while she was talking.

Another area she worked on was her voice. She learned to better project her voice and to speak with deeper tones. She practiced emphasizing certain words to add more variety. She also added impact by accenting her gestures—not enough to look like she was faking them, but just enough to make them more noticeable.

To overcome her small stature, she tried standing up and moving around when she was speaking for any length of time. At first, it felt a little awkward, but she told me, "Nobody has made a comment about how strange it is that I get up every time that I speak. They don't seem to notice."

Her "convincability," as she calls it, has grown tremendously since she began working on it in the ESE course.

"Now," she says, "they just can't miss me."

It can be a very big jolt when you see yourself as others do but it can make all the difference in the fine tuning you can do with that knowledge.

"Don't Do That . . . ."

I'm sure you remember the old Vaudeville gag about the guy who goes to the doctor with a sore arm.

"It hurts when I do that, Doc," he complains.

"Then, don't do that," the wise doctor prescribes.

Breaking away from the talking head and stick body reaction is not quite that simple, but in a later chapter, I'll give you some very effective techniques you can use to overcome the discomfort of being in front of a group.

First, let's look at how you can break free from the lectern and give your audience a show they'll never forget.

How To Project The Full Power Of Your Personal Presence

Robert H. Collins, III, was president of Getty Synthetic Fuels in Los Angeles when I first met him.

Bob is the kind of executive who can get people to give their best to his causes. One-on-one, he comes across as having a very astute mind and a powerful personality. He's a tactful and charming leader and has a great sense of humor. The other participants in the ESE course loved him and almost instantly began looking up to him.

But a strange thing would happen to this charismatic, effervescent, warm man when he stood up in front of a group. His magnetic personality rolled up like a window shade. He came across as an eagle-eyed, intimidating, cold, almost ruthless presenter. It was as if he were two different people.

The reason he lost his charm was that he read virtually everything he presented. He'd hang onto the lectern as if it were a battle shield. He'd look up fleetingly every now and then, almost as if he were checking to make sure everybody was paying attention.

We worked extensively on freeing Bob up, getting him away from the written manuscript. We weaned him with notes that would help him flow from idea to idea and express himself more extemporaneously. We worked on freeing up his eyes, his gestures and his body movements, and helped him get away from the podium.

Now, he loves to move around the room while he speaks because it gives him more personal contact with members of the audience. He finds that it makes him more believable and persuasive to move among the people.

"I feel like I'm talking to one person at a time," he told me, "like I have personal contact with each individual and I can tell exactly how each person is receiving me."

I asked Bob what the one-on-one contact with the audience had done for his own feelings of discomfort and nervousness about speaking. "I can't tell you how it's boosted my feeling of confidence. It's given me a whole new freedom. I'm having so much more fun as a presenter."

This freeing up has also enabled him to project much more clearly and persuasively his ideas and opinions on a personal contact level, he says.

How To Blend With Your Audience
Without Losing Your Identity

The most crucial element of connecting with your audience is *identification.* Before people will listen to what you have to say, they have to connect with you as a human being. The moment they can identify with you, the more interesting you become.

I remember some years ago turning on my television set and seeing some guy talking about relationships. I plopped down on a sofa and started flipping through a magazine.

"Who is *this* guy?" I thought as I glanced up at the screen. He was not what I'd call physically attractive or impressive, and he was violating all the traditional rules for public speaking, especially for television. He was dressed casually and had a rather scraggly beard, and he kept stroking it. Still, there was something intriguing, maybe even captivating, about him.

Once, when I glanced up, the camera pulled back and I could see this huge audience, hundreds of people, all sitting on the edges of their seats. Then the cameras started zooming in for close-ups of faces and I could see that these people were totally wrapped up in every word the man was saying.

"Who *is* this guy?" I wondered as another camera gave a long shot of the stage. He'd pulled off his coat and slung it over the back of a chair, then sat down on the stage.

As I listened, he talked about needs we all feel—the craving to be loved, to be appreciated, to be recognized, to have people be sensitive to us and accept us as we are.

Before long I was yelling, "Honey! You've got to come in here and see this guy!" It wasn't until the end of the show that I learned that "this guy" was Leo Buscaglia.

I've watched Leo many times since then and I'm convinced he's one of the most fantastic communicators in America. Why? Because he has the guts to be real, he comes across as sincere and caring, and he talks about the things people care a great deal about.

"Oh, I Could Never Do That!"

I know what you're thinking: "Oh, I could never do that with an audience!"

Good! I'm not suggesting you should try to be like Leo Buscaglia. It's natural for him and it fits his audience, his environment and his purpose.

That's the whole point: don't try to be like anybody else. Get real! Get in touch with the physical characteristics and personality traits that best reveal who you are as a human being and learn how to project them more emphatically and on a larger scale.

The other side of the coin is to get in touch with your audience and find ways to show that you identify with their feelings, their needs and their concerns. Find out what they want most, what they fear most, what they stay up nights worrying about.

It's this simple: you have to take the reality of who you are to the reality your audience is experiencing at the moment, before you can lead them to what you'd like to share with them.

The Golden Key To Connection

You've probably seen people do some crazy things to try to connect with their audiences. I sure have. I've seen them parade on stage with a bikini-clad model, or open with a smutty story, or wear a fish tie, or stumble all over the place on their way to the platform.

In certain settings, you might get some laughs this way, but it won't help you connect with your audience at a gut level. Why? Because you're calling attention to yourself, not to what you have to say.

The golden key that unlocks the minds and hearts of any audience is sincerity, and you can't fake that.

How much do you care about the people you're speaking to? How much do you care about the message you're trying to get across? How sincerely do you want your message to impact on the lives of the people before you?

Oh sure, there are some techniques you can use to break through in a constructive way. And, in the chapters that follow, I'm going to give you plenty of specific techniques for establishing and maintaining in-depth contact with your audience. But, if you don't really care about people and about impacting positively on their lives, all those techniques will do is call attention to your insincerity.

It's Halftime In The Locker Room

The President of the United States has to think about connecting, and he does. The board chairman of General Motors discovered the hard way that he had to be concerned about it, and he is. Even the premiere of the Soviet Union has come to realize how crucial it is to connect with people if he wants to get anything done.

"I don't have to worry about all that business," you might be thinking, "people have to listen to me because I'm the boss . . . they don't have any choice."

I'm going lay it all on the line with you, just like I do when I'm coaching top executives, because I feel so deeply about this issue of really connecting with your audience.

Maybe you think you are too busy to take the time to learn the mechanics of connecting with your audiences. But, the fact is, you didn't get to where you are, and you won't get to where you want to go, by doing this in a half-hearted way. It's like your mother always told you: "If it's worth doing, it's worth doing well."

Looking Ahead

In Chapter One I told you why it was worth doing, and in this chapter I've explained how to do it well. Now, let's start mastering the specifics that can enable you to get out there and play this game like a champion.

CHAPTER THREE

SET YOUR STRATEGIC FOCUS

"Leadership is the art of getting someone else
to do something that you want done
because he wants to do it."
—*Dwight David Eisenhower*

There is enough power in a 100 watt light bulb to cut through a one-inch bar of steel when that light energy has been focused into a laser beam.

Of course, I'm glad the rays of a light bulb are so diffused they have no cutting power. I'd just as soon not have a hole cut in my ceiling or in a book I'm trying to read.

But, if I have to go to a clinic for an operation on my eyes, or to a hospital for heart surgery, I want the physician to have the sharpest and most accurate laser beam there is.

What does that have to do with speaking? More than you might think.

I'm sure you've seen and heard plenty of light bulb speakers—they scatter information all over the place and when they're turned off, the information quickly disappears, leaving no lasting effects.

But good speakers use the laser technique. They focus and amplify their information and ideas in a strategic direction.

Mastering Generalship

Napoleon Bonaparte understood the strategic dimension of speaking. Once, when his troops were bogged down in Africa after endless months of what seemed like fruitless marching, they became so lonely and discouraged that they started planning a mass desertion just before the great general was planning to launch the critical attack he'd spent months positioning his army to mount.

Napoleon assembled the troops and gave them a rousing oration. He told them, "The eyes of all of France are looking down upon you tonight." Then, he asked them to think about their wives, their sweethearts, their parents and their children, whose very lives lay in their hands at that moment. He ended his speech with a strong appeal to patriotism, assuring them that they could carve a niche for themselves in the honorable history of their native land by staying for the fight.

To a man, the troops stayed and fought and won.

That's literally what strategy means—generalship. It means the artful managing of resources to defeat an enemy and gain an end.

And, heaven knows, all of us face enough enemies to keep us from reaching whatever goals we may be aiming for as communicators. There are enemies like apathy, confusion, competition, ignorance, conflict, misunderstanding, envy and many more.

So, if we know how to use it, speaking is much more than a trivial pursuit. That's especially true in the business and professional arena where activities have to be evaluated by the impact they have on the ever-present bottom line.

But the key to making it work for us is focus. To be effective, we have to focus our objective, our audience, our content and our presentation. Let's take a closer look at each of those four focuses and how they can help you get more of what you want, every time you speak.

Focus Your Objective

Novices always start preparing for a speech by trying to figure out what to say, but veteran speakers begin by deciding precisely what they want their speech to accomplish.

The first step is to imagine that your speech has just ended and your audience is doing precisely what you want them to do. Then you ask yourself, what exactly would I like them to do?

Isn't it amazing how many top professionals, people who wouldn't dare operate without clear objectives in any other business function, go into one speech after another without the slightest thought of what they hope to accomplish.

If you don't know what you want a speech to accomplish, the best you can hope to do is to leave your audience like little Lord Fauntleroy, who jumped on his horse and rode off in four directions at once. At best, you might get them so excited they'll want to do something, but they won't have the foggiest notion as to what that should be.

Focusing Objectives: The Qualitative Side

In the early stages, it may be enough to visualize your audience rising to their feet and giving you a standing ovation. I've never yet seen a good speaker who didn't have some ego lurking around inside. And, I don't care how good you are, it's a great boost to your confidence to see an audience break into uproarious applause.

But, after you've been at it awhile, you'll probably realize that applause can be like racing a car's motor while the transmission is in neutral—it sounds powerful, but it doesn't go anywhere.

You'll eventually want to start shooting for some deeper and more lasting qualitative results; like making sure your audiences understand, and believe, and care about your goals.

Your objective may be as simple as making the audience have a good time or creating positive feelings toward your organization or cause. In certain settings these are very valid objectives. If fun and goodwill are what the occasion calls for, it's best to forget about your hidden agendas and structure your presentation to be as entertaining as you can make it. If you can't bring yourself to simply entertain people, it's best not to speak on such occasions.

Focusing Objectives: The Quantitative Side

The most common problem with executive speakers is that they try to accomplish far too many objectives, or objectives that are far to big, with each speech.

For example, the CEO of a company that's been under fire for two decades for polluting the environment may want to go on one television talk show and "set the record straight, once and for all." That's like trying to build an office tower overnight.

Another common mistake is to think of each presentation as an isolated event, a one-shot deal that has little or nothing to do with anything else the speaker is doing.

I've known professionals who seize every opportunity to hold forth on subjects that are totally unrelated to their expertise. At best, that is unproductive and, at worst, it can be damaging to your career. An insurance executive, for example, who becomes widely known as an expert on the fine art of sailing yachts is just further enhancing the perception that insurance companies are getting rich by gouging the public.

In the business and professional arena, speeches and presentations work best when they are focused on short-term objectives that are rooted firmly in long-term goals, and geared specifically to the perceptions of the audiences that will hear them.

Let me illustrate with an example. Let's say your company has made some long-term investments in technology and that the strategy is creating some real problems. You're taking a licking with stockholders because your profits are down, employees are upset because they fear the changes, your customers are concerned that quality is slipping, and your community is worried about the impact the new technology will have on the environment.

There is no way your CEO is going to dispel all those anxieties by a speech or two to the local Rotary Club. On the other hand, the worst thing you can do is to be mute.

You need to develop a long-term strategy with clear and specific goals, then launch a speaking blitz that puts your key executives before the right groups over an extended period of time. Your executives need to be properly coached so that their presentations have a realistic, quantitative objective contributing directly to your long-range goals.

Even if your organization is small, you'd be amazed at what you can accomplish by setting a clear objective, tied to your long-term goals, for each speech you make.

If you don't know precisely what you want a speech or presentation to accomplish, how can you structure it to achieve anything worthwhile? You're like many of the sales-people I've been called in to train and coach over the years. They make dazzling presentations, a lot of them, but they're ineffective because they never get around to asking for the order.

Once you know precisely what you want to achieve with each speech, it is much easier to put the speech together in a way that will accomplish your objective.

Focusing Objectives: The Personal Side

Aside from your role as a representative of your organization, I assume you have certain career and personal goals that are important to you. We've already seen how much your presentation skills can do for (or against) your career. But have you considered exactly how you will use speaking to enhance your career growth?

Obviously, for example, if you're presenting a new idea to a group of key executives, the most powerful way to boost your standing is to make an effective presentation.

Yet, beyond that, there may be a number of worthwhile objectives to consider. Suppose, for instance, that you are so convincing that the bosses buy the idea; then it bombs. Is there a way you can be convincing, without getting identified as the person who came up with the idea that cost the company a fortune? That might be a very good objective.

If you are adept at fielding questions, an objective might be to showcase that skill during your presentation. If you can argue both sides of an issue, you might prove it by structuring your presentation that way. If you have enough savvy to understand the big picture, you can highlight your macro-thinking ability by showing how your ideas fit an overall agenda.

The important thing to remember is that you can accomplish a very specific objective with each speech, but usually only one, and only if you focus clearly on that objective.

Focus Your Audience

Evangelist Billy Graham, who for more than two decades has shown up on the list of the 10 most recognizable people in the world, once told a story that emphasizes how difficult it can be to focus an audience.

Graham was scheduled to address a group of students at the Southwestern Baptist Theological Seminary in Dallas. On the morning of his address, heavy cloud cover rolled in and forced the Dallas Airport to close. When the time came for him to speak, his airliner was still circling over the city, waiting for the clouds to clear up.

"I'm afraid that's the way it is too often with us preachers," Graham later told the future ministers at a rescheduled meeting. "While the people sit on the ground and wait for us to give them the truth, all we're doing is circling around in the fog."

It's bound to be that way when you don't have your audience clearly in focus. The best you can hope to do in this situation is to throw out enough variety so that everybody can find *something* to identify with.

Probably the most valuable asset any speaker can have is a sensitivity to and awareness of what an audience cares most deeply about. In the absence of that, we end up talking about what *we* care most about, in terms that have meaning only to us.

It is totally unproductive, for example, to talk to employees about the company's need for higher profits, or better quality, or more productivity without showing them how those things impact on them. The response will be "So what?"

Do Your Homework

Long before you begin to prepare your presentation, even before you choose your topic, you need to carefully study your audience and know who they are.

As a professional speaker, I have developed an in-depth questionnaire which enables me to get a complete picture of each audience I will be addressing. By asking the meeting planner certain questions, I can usually determine common interests and concerns the group shares, what they are looking for out of the session and what turns them off. I also want to know in advance about the rest of the program and how I will be positioned in relation to other speakers and events.

In fact, there are certain basic questions I will ask before I even accept an invitation. If I decide that I will not be able to get through to an audience, I won't accept the invitation, no matter how much the fee might be. I would, for instance, turn down an invitation to speak to a group of people who will have just been treated to a two-hour cocktail party. Nobody can get through to an audience that is soused, and I have better things to do than spend my time trying.

It always helps to have a complete profile of the audience and the circumstances under which you'll be presenting.

You can really get yourself into hot water by not knowing enough about your audience. One of my clients told me about one of their presenters—a big-time professional, no less—who came striding into their meeting room, just in time for his presentation. As he spoke, he kept making deferential remarks to a group of men who were sitting near the front. He talked about how it was clear that they were providing good leadership and that the company's progress showed that they were men of vision. He completely ignored a woman and her daughter who just happened to be the owners and chief operating officers of the outfit. Needless to say, the women were livid, and rightfully so. This speaker effectively closed the door to a very lucrative client because he didn't do his homework.

Another tactic I use is to make a point to get to the location of any presentation well in advance. I check out the environment and pick up the rhythm of what's happening with the group before I go on stage. If necessary, I can adjust my presentation to fit the circumstances and the mood of the people.

Gerry Kenny, the man you met in the first chapter, used this approach to set up his presentation to the Senate committee. He went over to the Capitol and watched six or eight other presenters before he went in to make his appearance. The professional lobbyists who were working with him couldn't understand why he would want to waste time like that. But Gerry knew exactly what he was doing, and it paid off. If he hadn't watched the others, he would probably have been given the same brush off they all got.

Whatever methods you use, the impact of your speech will be directly proportional to how clearly you have your audience in focus.

But let me throw out one caution: no matter how thorough a job you do researching and analyzing your audience, you are going to be off-base sometimes. That's why I've included a complete discussion later on how to read your audience, once you're standing in front of them.

Focus Your Content

Once you know precisely what you want to achieve and you have your audience clearly in focus, you are ready to decide exactly what you should say to accomplish your objective.

If your objective is fairly constant and your audiences are always similar, focusing your content may be little more than adjusting your stories and language to fit the nuances of each group. But watch out, it's easy to get into a rut and treat all audiences and occasions the same way. If you do that, don't be surprised if your audiences start going to sleep on you.

How To Avoid Being A Bore

"The best way to be boring is to tell everything," said Voltaire, and he's right.

Most experts know infinitely more about their subjects than their audiences could ever grasp or even care to know. (I'm assuming, of course, that you won't be talking on topics you don't know anything about.)

Therefore, the key to focusing your content is to select precisely the right information, and there are two criteria you can always count on to help you do that.

First, ask yourself, "Exactly what do they need to know to do precisely what I want them to do?" If you can accomplish your objective without telling something, don't tell it. But make sure you include all the vital information people need to decide in favor of your objective.

That means you have to know what people understand and believe before you can decide what to tell them. It is hazardous to your effectiveness to assume that your audience understands everything you know. Remember, what you know so well, others may not know at all. It's also risky to assume that people believe as you do, just because it's so obvious to you. Always test your assumptions before you select your content.

The second criteria for focusing your content is to ask, "What will have the most impact with my audience?" What information will they find most convincing? What information will they be most receptive to hearing? How will they connect it with other information they already have? What objections will they have to my ideas and how can I best answer those objections? What is the one key issue that must be settled in their minds before they'll buy into my ideas, and how can I best settle it? What is the one thing I can say that is most likely to make them do what I want done, and how close can I come to saying it?

In other words, you choose the information that will get the job done for you; not simply a string of points that fit together into a neat outline.

One important point to remember about selecting your content is that some things are conspicuous for their absence. GM's Chairman Smith, for instance, created a great deal of negative feeling among the company's employees by consistently failing to mention the contributions the work force was making. He now says it was an oversight, but employees took it as a snub. Make sure you don't leave the things that need to be said, even if you have to omit some things you'd like to say.

Focus Your Presentation

It is only when you have your objective, your audience and your content clearly in focus that you can begin to decide how you will put it all together for maximum impact.

Focusing your presentation, as we will see later, is arranging your content in the most compelling way and customizing both your content and presentation tactics.

Good speakers—laser beam speakers—always meet you where you are, reach out and take your hand, then lead you smoothly to where they want you to go. When they finish, you may be mentally and/or emotionally miles from where you started, but you don't feel disoriented because you know how you got there.

Conversely, light bulb speakers jump around all over the place. And, when they finish, you haven't the faintest idea of where you are and you may even wonder where the speaker is.

Focus Your Positioning

The first, and most crucial, decision you'll have to make in focusing your presentation is how you will position yourself. I'm not talking about physical positioning (if, or where you'll stand) but mental/emotional positioning—the position you want to occupy in the minds and hearts of your audience.

Your positioning is the way your audience thinks and feels about you during and after your presentation. Do you want them to think of you as a powerful and dynamic leader who has everything under control? As a warm and caring friend who has their best interests at heart? As an authoritative expert who knows your stuff better than anyone else in the world? As a fiery motivator who knows how tough things are but who also knows how much latent power we all have inside us? Or, maybe you want to come across as a tough cookie who can't be pushed around.

Every one of the above positions, and a host of others, can be used effectively as a focusing strategy.

Most speakers don't think much about positioning. They think it's enough to "tell it like it is and let the chips fall where they may." Besides, as they'll tell you, "People are going to think pretty much what they want to think, and there's nothing you can do about it."

But astute presenters figure out exactly how they want to come across to their audience, then they carefully orchestrate the whole process to reinforce that positioning. As a result, they are able to accomplish very specific objectives.

Let me caution you not to get carried away with positioning and overdo it, or try to come across in a way that does not fit your personality. For example, if you are a slow talking southerner, don't imitate a Philadelphia lawyer. Over time, you might find it helpful to speak a little faster and minimize your accent, but it takes a lot of practice and will make you look like a fake in a one-shot effort.

Another example would be trying to come across so much like an expert that you cannot be proven wrong, even if you are. A friend of mine, an insurance executive, once told me about listening to Chrysler's Lee Iacocca make a speech and field questions. During the questioning, someone in the group pinned him to the wall about a statement he'd made. My friend said that Iacocca kept insisting, to the point of appearing arrogant, that he was right, although everybody in the place knew he was wrong.

You don't help your positioning by trying to appear more knowledgeable than you really are.

Looking Ahead

If you want to get what you came for, every time you speak, you'll need to become a master at focusing—focusing your objective, your audience, your content and your presentation.

When you have carefully set your strategic focus, you are ready to begin preparing the actual tactics you will use to get your message across. And, that's what we'll look at next.

CHAPTER FOUR

DON'T JUST TALK: ORCHESTRATE!

"He draweth out the thread of his verbosity
finer than the staple of his argument."
—*William Shakespeare*

"**O**ur next speaker is Ted Santon, CEO of Lincoln Financial Services and Insurance Company in San Francisco," announced the meeting facilitator for an industry gathering at the University of San Diego.

"When I heard my name called, I froze," Ted later told me. "I said to myself, 'I can't get out of this chair!'"

Anybody who knew Ted Santon at that time would have told you that he could hold his own in almost any environment. He always came across like an executive's executive: calm, confident, cordial, amusing, sometimes even funny, and always in control. But the idea of standing in front of a small group, not to mention a large one, made him turn to jelly inside.

The more his introducer talked about Ted's expertise and how fortunate they were to have him speak at their meeting, the more he felt riveted to his chair.

"I thought that I actually would not be able to get out of that chair," he confessed.

Of course, he did somehow manage to get out of his chair and he did make his presentation. You don't build the kind of successful track record Ted had built for himself and his company by backing away from opportunities just because you feel anxious about them. Afterward, people came up and congratulated him on his performance.

But Ted knew he had been so distracted by his own discomfort that he hadn't even come close to doing his best. He
also knew that he was going to be doing more presentations
as he moved his company forward.

A top-flight business leader, Ted Santon knew that less
than his best would not be good enough. So, he enrolled in
our Executive Speaking Experience to conquer his lack of
self-confidence in front of groups.

During the course, Ted made an interesting discovery that
enabled him to feel much better about his speaking and to be
much more effective as a presenter. After the ESE, he made
speeches more often—not just responding to invitations,
but actually seeking them out.

Recently, he was invited to give the keynote address at a
conference in Hawaii. This time, he sat on the edge of his seat
during the introduction, couldn't wait to get on stage and
spoke quite effectively for about an hour.

"The opportunity was just mind-boggling," he said, "and it
felt so good to be able to stand in front of a large group like
that and handle it confidently."

That's quite a turnaround for a CEO who sat frozen in his
chair when his name was called. What did Ted discover that
made the difference? Let's explore it in this chapter.

Orchestrating The Whole Process

The secret to feeling confident, having personal presence
and achieving your objectives before any size group is to
orchestrate everything that impacts in any way on the
whole process. In other words, don't wait for things to
happen. Take charge and create the results you want to
happen.

Now, that can be a real challenge, but it's not as hard as
you might think, for three very big reasons.

First, I'm assuming that you are the kind of person who is
accustomed to taking charge in many areas of your life.
Orchestrating a presentation before a group involves func-

tions you're already familiar with, like: analyzing, planning, decision-making, problem solving, monitoring, and so on.

You don't need to start from scratch and learn a whole new way of thinking and acting. You can adapt something you've been doing for so long that it's probably become second nature. You can apply your own personal style to speaking.

Second, you have systems, skills and techniques which enable you to take charge in your position or profession.

Let's say, for instance, that you're a physician. You don't wait for your patients to tell you what they think is wrong with them and suggest their own treatments. Even if they try to do that, you resist it and follow the structured procedures that you know will produce the best results for them.

As we go along, you're going to learn some systems, skills and techniques that will enable you to guide the presentation process in much the same way.

Third, your audience expects and wants you to take charge. They want you to do well.

Think about your own experience at meetings. Can you imagine saying to yourself, "Boy, I hope this speaker is a dud!"? Of course not. You might say, "I sure wish I didn't have to attend this meeting." Or you might even fear that a speaker is going to bomb. But very few people go into a meeting with the desire to be bored to death.

If you're like most people, you want to at least be amused, informed and perhaps even inspired.

So, when you're the presenter, the best way to make a hit with your audience and fulfill their expectations is to take charge and run the show.

Drill Sergeants Need Not Apply

You don't have to be aggressive or arrogant or dogmatic to orchestrate the presentation process. In these days of the "what's-in-it-for-me?" mentality, drill sergeant tactics won't endear you to any audience.

This is true whether you are speaking to employees, to community groups or to your peers. It's especially true if you're presenting to your superiors, to stockholders or to customers.

Learning to orchestrate involves discovering what works best for you with your audiences, how to use what you can do best, how to avoid what you do poorly, and how to make everything contribute to your objectives for each presentation.

So, what does it mean to orchestrate the process? And how do you go about it?

Pre-Planning: The Key To Orchestration

When a concert orchestra conductor steps in front of an audience, it's too late to figure out what to do and how to do it. The baton goes up, an awesome silence falls across the concert hall and everything seems to hang in suspense.

When the timing is perfect, the conductor drops the baton and the musicians respond in perfect synergy.

The conductor knows the score, knows precisely what to expect from each section, knows which passages need special attention, and has a clear and practiced strategy for producing each of the effects that will combine to create a magnificent symphony. If something goes wrong, the conductor has a ready-made recovery plan.

It's the same when you orchestrate a presentation. You know what to expect from your audience, you know precisely what you are going to say and do, you know how you're going to present each idea, and you have a clear and practiced strategy for creating each effect you want to produce. And, if something goes wrong, you have a "Plan B" that will get things back on track.

All of this results from doing a complete job of pre-planning and preparation. And, you use the same basic techniques you use in planning and preparing for any other important activity.

In the last chapter, we said we must focus four things to be effective: our objective, our audience, our content and our presentation. Let's explore how pre-planning and preparation can enable us to do this.

(1) *Prepare your objective*—Decide precisely what you want to accomplish. Ask these questions:

- Why do I want to speak to this group? Why now?

- Why would this group invite me? Why would they listen to me?

- If I called this meeting, exactly why did I call it?

- What are they expecting me to say and do?

- What response would I like to get from this group immediately? In the long run?

- Is it realistic to expect that response?

- What would keep me from getting that response?

- Exactly how will I know that I am getting the response I want?

(2) *Prepare for your audience*: Do a detailed audience profile by asking these questions:

- How much do they know about me? About my topic?

- How interested are they in my topic?

- How do they feel about my position on the topic?

- What kind of language are they most familiar with? Professional jargon? Complex terminology? Street language?

- Who are the key influencers in the group? How do they feel about my objective and topic?

- Will the key decision-makers be here? Can this audience

give me the response I want?

- Who will make-up the audience? How many people? Gender mix? Ages? Educational level? Socio-economic status? Career and professional mix?

- What will the physical setting look like? Feel like? Time of day? Facilities? Seating arrangement?

- What will be the nature and purpose of the meeting? Where and how do I fit in?

- What events are scheduled before and after I speak? How will this audience most likely feel at the moment I am introduced to speak?

- What other speakers have they liked? Why? Disliked? Why? What does that suggest to me?

(3) *Pre-plan to focus your content*: To prepare your content, ask these questions:

- Do I already know enough about the topic to be credible and informative to this audience?

- What additional data will I need? How can I find it most quickly and easily?

- Which of my ideas need support materials and where can I get them?

- What are my three or four key points? How can I state them most succinctly? How can I support them most effectively?

- What's the most compelling arrangement for my main points? If my purpose is to entertain, what is the most amusing or interesting way to put my key points together?

- What are the best stories I can use to reinforce my arguments? Do they really reinforce the points? If not, where can I find better stories?

- What metaphors or symbols can I use to aid in retention?

- What material can I delete, without losing impact? Are there any holes I need to fill?

(4) *Pre-plan your presentation*: To get the best results, plan what you want to say and how you will say it. To plan every aspect of your presentation, ask these questions:

- What is the best technique I can use to gain the attention of my audience and direct it toward my objective?

- How will I get my audience involved with me? With my content?

- How will I monitor their comprehension and acceptance of my ideas?

- How can I tell if I'm losing their attention and how will I get it back?

- How much time will it take to cover each point?

- What will I do if my time is cut short? or extended?

- What, specifically, will I be asking them to do? How will I know they have agreed to do it?

- What equipment will I have available? Is it adequate? How can I be sure it will work properly? Who will operate it?

- What visuals can I use to reinforce my points? How will I use them?

- Would it help to have a handout? How will I put it together and how will I present it?

- What is the most effective way for me to close the presentation?

- How will I test my ideas and presentation strategies in advance? What specific feedback will I be looking for?

- When and how will I rehearse my presentation?

In a nutshell, you use the same careful attention and forethought in preparing a presentation that you do in pre-planning any other important business or professional activity.

Sure, It Takes Time, But . . .

"Going through all that takes too much time," some might protest.

How much does being known as a capable presenter, one who is always worth hearing, matter to you? If you get nervous when you stand in front of a group, it must matter a great deal to you. Otherwise, you wouldn't care how you came across.

There is no shortcut. And, there are no born speakers. Those who speak with confidence, skill and impact know precisely what they are going to say and do, and exactly how they will say and do it, because they have taken the time to prepare.

Think about it from the perspective of your audience. In my estimation, wasting the valuable time of a group of people, because you are not willing to take the time to prepare, is the ultimate in arrogance. And, to publicly admit to an audience that you didn't take the time to prepare is adding insult to injury.

It's one thing to be called upon suddenly to stand and make a few remarks. Then, about all you can do is wing it. Nobody expects you to be prepared.

But, if people are interested and courteous enough to sit and listen to you, and if you accept their invitation, you owe it to them to take the time to prepare. It's just good manners.

The higher you go in your profession, the more people expect you to be able to articulate and present your ideas well.

Learning how to prepare and to pre-plan your presentations is a good investment. It's the only way you can effectively orchestrate a powerful performance.

How To Orchestrate Your Preparation

What's the first thing you do when you receive an invitation or assignment to give a high-level presentation? If you're like most business leaders, you gloat a little. You bask in the excitement of an opportunity to show your stuff and accomplish a worthwhile objective.

But, as my friend Dan Adams says, "Reality is an interesting concept." As the time draws closer, you find yourself less and less excited by the concept and more and more anxious about the reality. It begins to dawn upon you that you've got to get your act together and that time is running out.

Even top professional speakers gloat a little, but they also do something else. They set in motion a structured procedure to get themselves ready. They know that preparation is the master key to confidence.

Here are a set of 10 steps to a powerful, confident presentation:

Step One: *Clarify the assignment.* Precisely what are you being asked to do? What is your time limit? What are the specific objectives of the meeting planners? What conditions will you be under when you present?

Don't assume anything. For instance, if they say the meeting will last an hour, does that mean you'll have an hour to speak, or will you have only a fourth of it?

Ask questions and take copious notes. If you later realize you're not sure about something, go back and find out. Send a written confirmation of what you understand your task to be and how you plan to go about it.

Your goal for this step is to make clear that your expectations and theirs are identical.

Step Two: *Assess the audience.* Find out everything you can about the people who will hear you speak. Go back and ask the questions we listed earlier in this chapter. You'll also find more insights on how to assess your audience in a later chapter.

Remember, the better you understand your audience the more you can custom-fit your presentation to their needs, interests and concerns. When you can walk in knowing they are going to find you interesting, it's a great boost to your confidence.

Step Three: *Identify the topic.* If you're being assigned a topic, make sure you understand what that topic is and that it is something you can handle. Also, ask to be sent a copy of any notices sent to the audience in advance. That will protect you from misunderstandings; i.e., if they tell the audience to come expecting to have fun and you walk in with a serious agenda, you could be in big trouble.

Usually, you will be given a broad topic based on your expertise. It's up to you to narrow that topic down to a bite-sized chunk. The more specific you can be, the greater the impact your presentation will have. For example, if you're an expert on marketing and are invited to speak on "marketing in the next decade," you could speak for days on that subject. It would be better to narrow it down to "six factors that will reshape the marketing of widgets in the next decade."

One excellent way to identify your topic is to keep sifting through all the things you'd like to say until you can come up with a topical sentence. Ask yourself: "If I could only say one sentence of a dozen words or less to this audience, what would I say?"

Keep in mind that you always have to balance what you want to say against what your audience wants to hear. The nearer your topic is to the top of their priority list, the greater their interest will be.

Step Four: *Specify your objectives.* Follow the guidelines in Chapter Three to determine precisely what you want your presentation to accomplish. Keep in mind that the more specific your objective is and the closer it is to the objectives of the group you're speaking to, the easier it will be to achieve.

Step Five: *Research the topic.* The amount of research you'll need to do will be determined by a number of factors: how much you and your audience knows about the topic, how detailed your topic is, what information you will need to achieve your objective, and how many times and how recently you've spoken on the topic.

One good approach is to gather as much reliable data as you reasonably can, then sift out the material you don't need. Just keep narrowing the information down until you have found the most pertinent and powerful facts to back up your opinions and arguments.

I suggest you set up a regular procedure for doing research, one that enables you to collect and evaluate the best information with the least amount of time and effort. If you often speak on five or six topics, you might set up file folders on each. Then, as you run across relevant information in your reading, you can simply put copies in the appropriate folders.

Make sure you find or develop plenty of stories, illustrations and metaphors to use throughout your presentation. They're like windows in a house—they let in light and fresh air.

You will seldom use all the information you collect, but that's okay. The better you understand your topic, the more confidently you can speak about it and the less likely you are to make mistakes. Besides, information is to a speaker like water in a tank. The more water there is in the tank, the greater will be the force at the faucet.

Step Six: *Organize your material.* After you become thoroughly familiar with all the material you've gathered, go back through it and select the three or four most important points your audience needs or might want to know. Write out those main points on index cards.

Now, sort through all the material to find the two or three bits of information you need to support each of your main points and put it into a stack under the appropriate main point cards.

Keep narrowing the information down until you have no more than three or four clear main points and two or three bits of information to support each of them.

Remember, as Voltaire said, "The best way to be boring is to tell everything." Your challenge is to select only the information you need—no more and no less—to accomplish your objective with your audience.

Step Seven: *Structure your presentation.* The easiest way to put together a good presentation is to think of it as having three distinct parts; a beginning, a middle and an ending.

Start with the middle. Arrange your main points in the most compelling order and decide whether to present them in a logical sequence or a psychological sequence.

Logical sequences work better when your primary objective is to inform or demonstrate. They include:

(A) Time sequence—putting points into chronological order

(B) Spatial sequence—putting pieces into locational relationships.

(C) Important elements sequence—listing ideas that are related but not connected.

(D) Problem-analysis-solution sequence—identifies problem, diagnoses causes and proposes a solution. Note: This one can also be used as a psychological sequence.

(E) Proposition-proof-conclusion sequence—states position, proves why it's true and interprets what it means.

Psychological sequences appeal to emotions and are used to persuade, sell or move people to action. They include:

(A) Known-to-unknown sequence—uses what the audience knows to lay a foundation for facts they are unfamiliar with. Good for teaching new concepts, procedures, products or services.

(B) Common-to-uncommon sequence—starts at a point of agreement and moves to an idea that is controversial or heretofore unacceptable.

(C) Belief-to-greater-belief sequence—good for deepening convictions and gaining greater support.

(D) Belief-to-action sequence—using convictions to motivate people to act or perform in different ways.

Once you have your main points sequenced, decide what support material and story you will use with each.

Prepare A Script

At this point, it might be helpful to write out the main body of your speech, starting with a rough draft and refining it to a polished script. Be careful to write like you talk, not like you write. There is a big difference! Keep reading it aloud to make sure every word and phrase is comfortable for you to say.

Once you're comfortable with the way it flows, read through it just like you will deliver it and see how long it takes you to make each main point. Add the main point segments, plus about 20% (for the opening and close), to get your total length. Make sure you can deliver the entire presentation in less than the allotted time.

Develop Alternate Plans

To beat Murphy's law (If anything can go wrong it will!), develop alternate plans. What happens if they tell you the meeting is running behind and you have to shorten your presentation by 25%, maybe even 50%? Can you simply drop one of your segments without serious damage? Can you leave out some support material under each point?

What happens if you have to speak longer? Do you have a few extra stories to tell? Can you add another main point and support it? Can you add a more detailed summary and review?

The important thing is to know exactly what you will do if the ground rules change on you at the last minute. "Stuff happens," as the youngsters say, and it can blow your confidence right out of the water if you're not prepared.

Plan Your Opening

A powerful opening should take no more than 10% of the total time of your speech's main body and must accomplish these four objectives:

(A) It should capture the complete attention of your audience.

(B) It should make the audience comfortable with you.

(C) It should introduce the topic and make the audience eager to hear what you have to say about it.

(D) It should set up your first point so you can flow right into it.

Avoid gimmickry and shock tactics unless you have had years of experience and know exactly how to make them work.

Plan Your Closing

The way your audience members think and feel when you say your last words will be the way they remember your presentation for months, maybe years. So it's vital to go out with a bang.

A good close should last about 10% as long as your main body and accomplish at least three major objectives:

(A) It should recap and reinforce your main points.

(B) It should make clear what action you want in response to your presentation and how people will benefit from that response.

(C) It should give people a tangible opportunity to give you the response you want.

Closing a speech is like closing a sale. You have to ask for the order if you want to make a sale.

Step Eight: *Prepare a speaking outline.* Fewer than one speaker in a million can read a speech convincingly and persuasively. And, maybe two in a million can and will memorize a lengthy speech. By far, a better approach is to internalize the script as you practice it, then work from a very simple outline. That way, you will come across as being extemporaneous but well prepared.

Write out an outline with brief reminders of your key points. Use them as you would use signs along an expressway. You glance at them and know immediately what to do.

Write the key reminders for each segment on a 3 X 5 index card. That way, you'll only have one each for your opening and closing, and for each of your segments—five to seven, altogether.

After a few run-throughs with your cards, you may be confident enough to leave them in a pocket while you speak and pull them out only if you bog down.

Step Nine: *Plan your collateral material.* Once you have planned your entire presentation, decide what aids you will use to clarify your points and help your audience remember what you've said. These include things like visual aids (slides, transparencies, videos, flip charts, etc.), exercises (things to do, to write, etc.) and handouts (outlines, bibliographies, copies of visuals, etc.).

Such tools are so vital that we will later devote an entire chapter to them. Here, we're concerned with the crucial step of planning them. These guidelines will help:

(A) Allow plenty of time for preparation. Slides and videos Might take 2-4 weeks to produce. Sweating a last minute delivery can wipe out any confidence the aids might give you.

(B) Be very specific in your planning. Prepare dummies for everything.

(C) Make clear who will be responsible for every aspect of preparation, and communicate clearly with each person along the way.

(D) Set deadlines far enough in advance so that you can run through several mock presentations using your visual aids.

(E) Line up all the equipment you'll need well in advance, and do a last-minute check to make sure everything works properly.

Well executed collateral materials can add tremendous punch. If they bomb, your presentation will go down with them, so cover all bases so that your collateral materials will add to your confidence, not detract from it.

Step Ten: *Rehearse.* As soon as any part of your presentation is complete, it's a good idea to start practicing on it. But make sure you allow enough time for at least three complete dress rehearsals. Your confidence and effectiveness rise in direct proportion to the amount of time you spend in quality rehearsal.

Of course, if you practice and practice at doing something wrong, you will learn how to do it wrongly very well. It's like trying to dig your way out of a hole.

Here are some helpful guidelines for quality practice:

(A) Practice infusing energy into your speaking from the earliest stages. Get so accustomed to being enthusiastic that it feels completely natural to you.

(B) Videotape the final dress rehearsals if at all possible. If not, at least practice in front of a mirror and with an audio tape recorder. If you have trouble maintaining eye contact or vocal quality in rehearsal, you are not ready to perform live.

(C) Get someone whose judgment you trust to critique your rehearsals and give you constructive feedback.

(D) Practice, at least once, your alternate plans, especially the one for shortening your presentation.

(E) Keep practicing until you can perform credibly in a hurricane.

Looking Ahead

Orchestrating the whole speaking process may seem like quite a challenge at first. But, after you've done it a few times, you'll find it much easier, and more pleasant, than struggling your way through your speeches.

If you do it well, the audience gets into the process and actually becomes an asset to you, rather than the liability it once was.

In fact, the more you can get your audience involved, the more help they will be to you and the more they will enjoy your presentation. How do you do that? We'll explore it in the next chapter.

CHAPTER FIVE

ORCHESTRATE YOUR AUDIENCE

"Show people what they want and they will
move heaven and earth to get it."
Frank Bettger

You have the power to make people sit up and listen intently to every word you say, every time you speak. This chapter will focus on how to use that power.

But first, think about this. Why don't people just automatically sit up and pay rapt attention when a speaker steps before them? The answer is quite simple:

People don't pay attention because they don't care as much about what the speaker is saying as they do about someone or something else that's on their minds at the moment.

Apathy in an audience is not so much indifference toward the subject or speaker as it is preoccupation with someone or something else. The minds of people who hear us speak are like a battleground, with many voices and concerns constantly fighting to gain the upper hand.

We don't *give* our attention, we only *pay* attention, and we will always pay it to the highest bidder. We invest our attention in the person, thing or event which we perceive as offering us the greatest value in return.

Powerful speakers know how to wrestle the attention of their audience away from whatever has seized it, and they hold it away from whatever competition arises.

In short, if you want people to pay attention to you, you must make them care a lot, at least for the moment, about what you have to say.

The first law of effective speaking is this: no real communication can take place until you have the undivided attention of your audience, and communication stops the moment you lose that attention.

So, why don't more speakers make their audiences care enough to listen intently? Again, the answer is simple:

Most speakers don't care as much about what's on the minds of people in their audiences as they do about what's on their own minds.

It's easy to see how speakers fall into the trap of being totally wrapped up in what they are saying. After all, to speak with high energy and enthusiasm about a subject, you have to care a great deal about it, probably more than anybody in your audience. In fact, the more you care about it, the more forcefully you can present it.

So, what are you supposed to do? Act as if it doesn't matter to you at all? No.

Try these two tested and proven strategies to strike a good balance between your enthusiasm for your content and your concern for the interests of your audience.

Strategy #1: Earn Their Attention

Good speakers always assume that any audience is at best only mildly interested in them and what they have to say, and at worst totally apathetic or even hostile. From that starting point, they set about to do whatever it takes to build and maintain rapport.

If I may paraphrase John Housman's famous line in the Smith-Barney commercial, "They gain attention the old fashioned way—they *earn* it!"

How can you do that? How can you make yourself supremely important and capture the dominant position in the minds of your audience?

Think about your own experience in personal contacts and with speakers. Why is it that you will not give one person the time of day, but you will spend hours with another person?

One reason is that all of us tend to like some people more than we do others. Let's take a look at what we like about them.

(A) *We like people who are warm and friendly.* We like people who smile, who laugh easily without being giggly, and who seem cordial. Most of us don't like people to be solicitous, but we do like them to practice good human relations.

(B) *We like people who make us feel good about ourselves.* We like positive, upbeat people who cheer us up instead of tearing us down. And, we like people who treat us with dignity and respect.

(C) *We like people who are easy to trust.* We quickly warm up to people who seem to be at ease with us, who look and act sincere, who seem like our kind of folks. We shy away from people who seem shifty, who never look us in the eyes, who make us tense when we're around them.

(D) *We like people who show an interest in us.* We like people who seem to like us and who pay attention to our needs and interests. We don't care much for people who seem all wrapped up in themselves.

In other words, we like people who are comfortable to be with. So, if you want your audience to invest their attention in you, loosen up and let all your natural warmth and charm come through. Let them see what a nice person you really are.

The second reason we freely spend time with some people is that we are convinced they have something worthwhile to say to us.

(A) *We pay attention to people who look important.* People

who dress, act and present themselves like VIPs usually get much more of our attention than those who look like nobodies.

(A) *We pay attention to people who talk about things we are interested in.* If we're wrestling with a problem or excited about an opportunity, we'll listen to anybody who seems to truly understand and be able to help us achieve our goals. We don't pay much attention to people who have no interest in our priorities and concerns.

(B) *We pay attention to people who know what they're talking about.* We're ready to listen when people have their facts right, when they have good insights and when their opinions have some substance. We have little time for people who are often in error but never in doubt.

(C) *We pay attention to people who have something of value to offer us.* We'll listen all day to people who can show us how to make more money, or save time, or improve the quality of our lives and relationships, provided that their ideas make sense to us. But we don't pay much attention to people who are out to con us, or whose ideas are so far out we can't connect with them.

(D) *We pay attention to people who respect our time.* We'll listen to people who get right to the point, who say things concisely and who think before they speak. We don't like people to ramble, to spout out half-baked ideas or to stumble around forever trying to say something.

We, just like our audiences, pay attention to people we feel have something important to say to us and who can say it well. And, the more important it seems to us, the more we are willing to pay attention.

Perceptions are what we're dealing with when we step in front of an audience. We must not only say something vitally important, we must look and act important, and speak in a way that convinces people it's important.

Now, here's the second solid strategy you can use to orchestrate your audience and make them sit up and pay attention to you.

Strategy #2: Customize Your Presentation

Sylvia Wessel, president of San Francisco-based Strategic Research, Inc., is brilliant in marketing research and designing programs for technical companies. As a knowledgeable and persuasive marketing expert, Sylvia knows how crucial it is to establish credibility when you're selling anything, especially ideas.

Sylvia, an ESE graduate, told me about one of the toughest challenges she ever faced as a speaker. She had to present the results of a major research project to a cynical, technically-minded group of sales executives for a leading semi-conductor manufacturer.

This company had earned a strong reputation for design integrity, so much so that their customers were willing to pay them much higher prices than the average in their field.

The firm had faced little competition until the Japanese began to rapidly invade their market with more support, better service and greater flexibility.

Sylvia's challenge was to present a new marketing concept to this large international firm, which had always been rather aloof and inflexible, even toward its vendors and customers. Competition was forcing them to open up and become more flexible in their dealings, but it was not an easy transition for them to make.

"These people had always prided themselves on their objectivity," she said. "But, in truth, they were anything but objective."

Of course, Sylvia had done her homework. She'd conducted in-depth market research and had worked with focus groups to gain insights into her findings. After months of study, she had come up with a design the company could use to measure and improve customer satisfaction on an on-going basis. She knew that her information and ideas could make a great deal of difference in the growth, maybe even the survival, of this company.

But she also knew that to break through the engineering mindset and get approval to proceed with her plan, she would have to present her content in a way that they could connect with it and grasp its significance.

"I knew my presentation had to be quantitative, not just qualitative," she said. "And, I needed to carry a lot of confidence and credibility into the meeting."

So Sylvia took all of her qualitative information and put it into quantitative form. She used graphs, charts, numbers and percentages to make her points. She customized her presentation to fit the mindset of her audience.

It worked. The cynics challenged every one of her figures, but she defended each with solid data. They questioned her assumptions and ideas, but she backed them up with logic. When it was over, they not only bought her design but were enthusiastic in implementing it.

Get Personal: Get Response

Customizing works. Why? Because the moment something becomes personal, it becomes interesting. And, the more personal it becomes, the more interesting it becomes.

To have maximum impact, your presentation must create the impression that it was created for only one audience and that it could only be delivered by you.

It is vital to find out everything you can about your audience before you begin preparing your presentation. And, it's never enough to say, "Oh, I've spoken to this group before so I know all about them." Conditions change, priorities change, and people change.

"My tailor is the only person I know who makes sense," said George Bernard Shaw. "He takes my measurements every time he sees me."

You not only have to take the measurements of your audience, you have to design every aspect of your presentation in a way that will enable them to personally identify with you and with what you say and do.

Here are some simple tactics that can help you do that.

(A) *Look like they look; only better.* We all listen more attentively to people whose appearance is similar to ours, especially if we are impressed with the way they present themselves.

Why is that true? It's because the way we look reflects the way we see ourselves and other people. If we look like people in our audience, they feel less threatened by us and are, thus, more receptive to what we have to say. And, if we are dressed similarly, but a cut above them, they tend to think we are sharp enough that they would benefit from listening to us.

The more we blend with our audience, the more readily they will open up to us.

There are, of course, some limits to blending. I once spoke to an association of wholesale grocers, at their annual meeting in the Cayman Islands. They came to my session in beach wear. Now, I'm pretty comfortable with my body, but I was not about to stand in front of a mostly male audience in a bathing suit and try to make a presentation on a business subject. Instead, I chose an elegant casual outfit.

A good rule of thumb is to dress similarly enough to blend in, but distinctively enough to look special.

(B) *Talk like they talk, only better.* As speakers, we are usually seen as visitors, not as insiders. That can add credibility. It's like the old saying: "An expert is a person with a briefcase, more than 50 miles away from home."

The guest status can, however, work against us by creating a communications gap. "How could an outsider possibly understand what life is like for us," people often think.

One good way to bridge that gap is to use the language

and symbols that are common to the group. Sylvia Wessel spoke in a quantitative idiom with the number crunchers. If your audience is arty, talk art; if it's technical, talk jargon; if it's laid back, cool it. If your audience ever says, "I don't understand," your credibility is in peril.

Is it condescending to try to match the language patterns of your audience? No! It's common sense. I like what Will Rogers said when a college professor criticized the folksy language he used in talking to the masses. His reply: "A lot of people who don't say 'ain't,' ain't eating." If you want people to identify with you, talk like they talk.

But watch out. One of the quickest ways we identify outsiders is by their accent, or by their failure to use our language correctly. You not only have to talk like your audience does, you have to do it better than they do. This may take practice but it does wonders for your credibility.

(C) *Talk about what they care about.* We listen to people who really understand us and care about our deepest concerns. Imagine yourself as a very disinterested member of your audience, then find ways to make your imaginary self care deeply about everything you will say and do.

Keep testing your statements against the cynical question: *so what?* You say that quality is off. *so what?* You say that costs are out of line. *so what?* You say your idea will revolutionize the way people think about our company or product. *so what?* What does all that matter to me?

When you can answer every *so what?* in a way that makes the greatest cynic say *"Now, I see why you're so excited,"* you are well on your way to making your audience sit up and pay attention to what you have to say.

(D) *Find out how they'd like to be; then paint a picture of them that way.* We pay attention to people who make us feel special, people who see our real value as human beings and understand just how capable we are.

A black minister named Jesse Jackson came surprisingly close to becoming the presidential candidate of the Democratic Party in 1988 by helping people see the best in themselves. All over America, large bi-racial audiences could be heard chanting to his cadence: "I am important!" "My vote matters!" "I am somebody!" He showed that he believed it, but more importantly, he made them believe it.

Speakers who consistently bring out the best in their audiences usually don't have much problem getting people to listen to them.

(E) *Find out what they would move Heaven and earth to get; then explain how you can help them get it.* Salespeople call it "targeting the hot button." It's the idea of finding the one benefit that really turns a prospect on and keying all discussions to that special interest.

In a very real sense, all public speaking is selling—selling ideas, beliefs or information. So the more you can apply your content to the greatest desires of your audience, the more likely they are to pay attention to you.

One trap many speakers fall into is assuming they know what people want most, only to find out later that they missed it by a mile. It's easy, for example, for executives to assume that what employees want most is more money. Yet studies consistently show that employees rank respect and appreciation above getting more money.

Find out what people want most. Ask them, then listen carefully to what they tell you. Show people how to take items off their worry lists, show them how you can help them fulfill their wishes, and they will gladly give you their interest.

(F) *Find their funny bones; then tickle them regularly.* I've never seen an audience fall asleep from laughing too much, but I've seen many audiences nod off (and do a lot of other things) from laughing too little.

But have you ever noticed that many of the speakers who consistently get laughs don't think of themselves as being funny; while many speakers who think they are hilarious seldom get a laugh? The difference is that the speakers who get good laughs understand and appeal to the sense of humor of people in their audiences. The duds only use lines and stories *they* think are funny. There is a big difference.

The key to making laughter work is to understand your audience well enough to know what they think is funny, regardless of whether or not you think it is.

As you mull over the humorous lines and stories you will use, ask yourself questions like these: "Why would they think that was funny?" "Why would that not be funny to them?" "Does that touch them where they live?" "Is that something they can laugh about?"

Incidentally, understanding your audience is a great way to avoid being offensive in your use of humor. A colleague of mine, a well-known professional speaker, once prepared about a dozen very funny one-liners about "Daisy the cow" for a speech he was to give to top executives of The Borden Company. Fortunately, he had enough savvy to try one of them on the meeting planner during their ride from the airport and was told promptly and sternly that "Daisy" is a "sacred cow" to the people at Borden. Wisely, he dropped the cow stories.

These days, with all the special interest groups, it is dangerous, even stupid, to use humor with overtones of racism, sexism, nationalism or anything that can be construed as discriminatory.

But don't worry. That leaves plenty of room for humor. One of the best, and safest, ways to be funny is to make yourself the brunt of many of your stories.

Looking Ahead

To get people to pay attention to you, orchestrate your

presentation. Customize your content, your style and your delivery to your audience. Make it fit them like a tailored suit.

Good speakers are like good conversationalists. They keep you interested by being interested in you. You gladly listen to their stories and their ideas because you can identify with them. And, after you've listened to them a while, you feel like you've learned something and enjoyed learning it.

Some speakers go beyond that. They seem to hold you spellbound by the way they deliver their messages. You can do that with your audiences, too, if you know how to project your own style. Let's explore how to do that.

CHAPTER SIX

ORCHESTRATE YOUR STYLE

"Of all the talents bestowed upon men, none is
so precious as the gift of oratory. He who enjoys
it wields a power more durable than that of a great
king. He is an independent force in the world."
—*Winston Churchill*

What it takes to connect with your audience is a genuine love for people, a passion for what you want to inspire them to do and the courage to reflect your own unique style of delivery.

When an audience senses from your delivery that you have those qualities, you can hold them in the palm of your hand and achieve your objectives. Why? Because you grab them by the heart, not just by the head. It's the difference between orchestrating your delivery and merely giving a presentation.

Let me illustrate that critical difference, then we'll focus on the mechanics of how to do it.

When John F. Kennedy made his maiden speech before the U.S. Senate on May 18, 1953, he was anything but inspiring. Actually, most observers felt it was a terrible speech.

Oh, he had plenty of facts, he had solid data to back up his claims and he had clear, maybe even brilliant, ideas about how to solve the problems he cited. And he was all business—no stories, no humor, no human interest appeals; just straight to the bottom line.

As historian James MacGregor Burns later noted, the young senator's speech sounded more like a Harvard Business School lecture on economics than a rousing call to action.

Kennedy promised his aides and colleagues he would do better in the future, and he began an intensive study into the high art of connecting with people. He read books on speaking, worked with private coaches and practiced diligently.

By the late-'50s, audiences all over America were hanging onto his every word, the media were lifting pithy phrases and sound bites from every speech he gave and he was forging a new definition for the term "campaign debates."

When he stood before the American people to give his inaugural address on January 20, 1961, he was as warm as the weather was cold. His head was no longer buried in his prepared text, his voice was sincere and earnest and his eyes connected frequently through a television lens with the eyes of his audience.

The vigorous young President sought to reach out and embrace all Americans with his declaration, "We observe today not a victory of party, but a celebration of freedom." He invoked the memory of their ancient forebears, then declared the challenge his audience faced that day: "The world is very different now. For man holds in his mortal hands the power to abolish all forms of human poverty—and all forms of human life . . . ."

As the speech went on, he mustered all his natural charm and sought to convey to people around the world what he believed the average American felt: "Let every nation know—whether it wishes us well or ill—that we will pay any price—bear any burden—meet any hardship—support any friend—oppose any foe—to assure the survival and the success of liberty."

Steadily, he worked his way to the punch line of the whole speech: "And so, my fellow Americans, ask not what your country can do for you, ask what you can do for your country."

After his speech, the polls showed that Jack Kennedy had touched the very soul of his nation and gained the respect of leaders around the world. Historians have called it perhaps the greatest inaugural address of this century.

Orchestration: The Critical Difference

Why did that inaugural speech have so much more impact than his first speech before the Senate? More than anything else, it was the style and focus of the delivery. He shifted his attention away from what he had to say and onto his audience. His goal was no longer to give a powerful speech but to connect with each individual who would hear him.

To connect with his audience, he spoke to their concerns and hopes, he exuded warmth and confidence and he made them feel the power of his personal presence.

That's what it takes to establish rapport with any audience we address—the genuine love and concern for people that causes us to want to reach out and touch them. And there is no way you can fake that; today's sophisticated audiences instantly see through insincerity.

Draw In The Individual

A most critical task in connecting with your audience is to carry on a dialog with each individual present. It is only when they "feel" you and know that you "feel" them that you can make them understand and care about your mission.

Dr. Robert Schuller's televised and personal appeals brought in more than $12 million in extra donations in less than 90 days when he set about to build his huge Crystal Cathedral in Garden Grove, California. Any way you cut it, that's powerful connection.

Watch Dr. Schuller work, sometime. As the camera backs away for a long shot, notice his grandiose gestures and listen to the resonant tone of his voice. When the camera zooms in close for a tight facial shot, you get the feeling he is talking directly to you.

That's his secret. He is able to make every person in a vast audience, both live and on television, feel that he is talking directly to them. He makes them feel that he understands their deepest needs and desires and that he cares about their most pressing concerns. Thus, he is able to move them to extraordinary response.

When I first started my speaking and coaching career as a Dale Carnegie instructor, I was immediately struck by the high level impact I could have on the people who heard me speak. Sure, I was frightened, because I was the first woman instructor and many key people in the company had serious doubts that businessmen would accept a woman in the role of coach and teacher. Although it was an excruciating challenge, I was spurred on by the discovery that I could actually change people's attitudes about life, that I could help them develop more self-esteem and improve their communications skills.

Now, many years later, I am more awed than ever when people tell me (some with tears in their eyes) that something they discovered in my course or in private coaching has opened up a whole new dimension of success and personal fulfillment for them. I say this to help you realize that we all have tremendous power to influence others by touching them where they live. We can move people with our speaking.

One of the most helpful techniques I've learned is to think of the whole delivery process as a dialog with the audience. Certainly, most of the time, you'll be doing most or all of the talking. But, if you're adequately prepared and execute with sensitivity, you can actually make your audience feel that they are having an in-depth conversation with you. Later in this chapter, we'll explore some specific techniques you can use to transform every speech into an in-depth dialog.

The Name of the Game Is Response

The whole point of speaking to groups, at least as a business function, is to sell your ideas convincingly and persuasively enough to get people to do things. After all, what good is it to have a great vision if you cannot inspire people to help you bring it into reality? What value do the greatest ideas have if no one understands them or cares enough to implement them?

But you can connect with people, you can make them understand what you know and believe, you can make them care enough to act.

Try a little experiment with me. Clap your hands vigorously three or four times and notice the sharp crack each time they come together. Now, raise your right hand about six inches and go through the same motion. There's nothing but silence as your hands slide past each other—failing to make contact. That's the difference between connecting and just going through the motions.

In the new corporate and professional arena, connecting deeply enough with people to get them to respond is not as easy as it might once have been. As we saw in an earlier chapter, people today are more caught up in their own concerns and priorities, they're jaded by too much hype, and they've heard the best.

In our increasingly connected world, executives are finding that they can no longer sit behind their desks and push buttons. Leadership no longer means ordering people around: they have too many options. Beautifully printed annual reports and prospectuses are no longer adequate as the sole connections with investors, memos and bulletins no longer get through to employees like they once did and corporate silence is interpreted by communities as callousness or lack of concern.

"If you can't communicate, you can't command." That's the consensus of more than 2,600 successful executives, professionals and entrepreneurs questioned by John T. Molloy and his associates.

It's this simple: if you want to lead today you have to be able to connect with people at a very deep level through public speaking, media presentations and tele-conferences. And, long before the magical year 2000, it will be absolutely essential to connect with people through closed-circuit hookups, videotapes and video-conferences.

The sad thing is that many executives and managers don't yet see how vital it is to make the people connection. They say things like: "Darn it! I don't have time to stand around talking to people . . . I've got a business to run!"

Yet many of those same would-be leaders complain about high turnover, about the difficulty of finding good employees, about dissatisfied customers and about restless investors. Somehow, they don't see that people no longer follow blindly after leaders just because others follow them.

To move people to action today, you must feel a passion for what you are doing and you must make others feel and care about your vision. If you don't show your excitement, nobody else will get excited.

So, if you believe that what you are doing is worthwhile (and I would bet you do), let me urge you to come out from behind those closed doors and show people who you really are and how much you care. You'll be amazed at how much more effective you will be when you throw the full weight of your personal power behind your efforts to influence, motivate and guide people.

Cash In On The Power Of Your Own Style

You don't have to abandon your own style or personality to sell, to communicate, to gain rapport, to turn people on. You don't have to speak like Winston Churchill or John F. Kennedy or Robert Schuller or Lynda Paulson.

In fact, the more fully you can be yourself, the more you can give people the freedom to be themselves with you.

One of the frustrations of writing a book is that I can't tell you how to find your own speaking style because it's so personal, it's so individualized. If we were face to face, I might be able to help you discover your communications assets and liabilities. But, even then, you'd have to get in touch with the strengths of your own personality and appearance and muster the confidence to let your own style come out.

All I can do here is to encourage you to discover who you are and to simply be your best self with your audiences—to master your own style, and to blend your expertise with your personal power of communication.

At least 99% of the people I work with are experts at what they do. I don't try to teach them how to be better experts. I only enable them to take what they already know and express it more effectively, to use what they know to influence or to inform.

Beyond Projecting An Image

Reflecting your own style runs much deeper than projecting an image. It's having the confidence to reveal your true self; to show emotion, to let people know you care, to be approachable.

I saw a good demonstration of this in one of my ESE courses with two men named Bob who managed different types of companies—one a construction company and the other a wine company.

The construction Bob was so tough and so in control of his emotions that for the first two days everybody thought he hated being there, and even hated them. Because he was trying to project an image of power and authority, he came across as intimidating, as angry, as almost defiant.

But the other Bob was the softest, warmest, most genuine, most approachable person in the whole class. Now, just because this guy was friendly and displayed a great deal of sensitivity, it did not indicate that he was weak. His approachability actually gave him more power with the people in the group.

On the last day of the course, the participants began to give constructive feedback to each other. When they came to Bob the builder, his tough-guy image generated a lot of comment.

"You know, Bob," one person said, "when you look at me like you're angry, I know you probably don't mean anything by it but it's intimidating. Your lip goes up like you're snarling, and I feel like you don't like me at all." Others tactfully expressed similar feelings.

"I didn't mean to imply that at all," Bob responded. "I never realized people saw me that way." There, in that neutral setting, he had experienced for the first time someone having the maturity and the freedom to tell him honestly how he was coming across.

As the session was winding down, he confessed that he had always tried to project a tough image because he feared letting people see his human side. When he dropped the image projection and began to just be himself, we could all see not only his sensitivity but his strength of character. His facade had been masking his power.

He went back to his company a better leader. His power had not been undermined, in fact, the opposite had occurred: he had discovered that his real self gave him more power with people than the image he'd always projected.

How To Cultivate Your Own Style

Developing your own delivery style is simpler than you might think. Mostly, it's identifying and abandoning the false fronts that hide your real personhood.

The crucial factor is not how you want others to see you; it's how they actually see you. For instance, what you interpret as projecting your professional expertise (by talking over everyone's head, for example) may be seen by others as trying to put them down. Or an inability to be open about the way you feel may come across to others as coldness, or lack of courage, or even insincerity.

Discovering how you come across to others, and how you can come across more genuinely, may have more impact on your ability to move an audience than all the techniques and gimmicks I or anyone could teach you.

Yet, making those discoveries can be tough to do. Coworkers and superiors may not be brave enough to tell you how they really experience you. They may not even know why they feel the way they do about you.

The best way I know to find out how you are received by others is to spend some time in a constructive environment with a small group of people who have nothing to lose by being open with you. Fantastic self-discovery can happen in this way and I know what an exciting change in effectiveness it creates. The important thing is that you somehow find out how you come across to others.

In the right environment, you can learn the mechanics of correcting those behaviors and habits that turn people off, and how to make the most of your personal assets.

If you remember only one thing from this book, let it be this: Don't abandon your own style or personality; let your most natural self come through. It's your greatest source of power with people.

How To Amplify Your Personal Style

Once you discover your delivery style, there are some ways you can emphasize it for even the largest of audiences. Here are some techniques that work very well with any delivery style.

It might be helpful to think of these tactics as tools to amplify your personal presence, much like a high quality sound system enables you to speak in a more natural voice and still be heard clearly.

Tactic #1: *Reflect your style through your introduction.* It's usually a good idea to write out your own introduction and request that it be followed closely. Make sure it reflects the style and content of your presentation and doesn't merely catalog all your achievements. Most people only want to know what they can expect and what qualifies you to present it.

Most introducers welcome a written introduction and it can solve two problems for you. First, it eliminates long, boring, sometimes embarrassing introductions. A good rule of thumb is one minute of introduction for 10 minutes of speech, then add 20 seconds for each subsequent 30 minutes of presentation.

Second, a written introduction enables you to set the stage properly for your presentation.

One thing more, don't spend a lot of time disclaiming all the glowing things in your introduction. It's unprofessional and either makes you look insincere or sounds like you're putting yourself down. Just turn toward your introducer, say a warm "Thank you," then turn back to your audience and get on with your presentation.

Tactic #2: *Involve your audience verbally from the word "go" and keep them involved.* The most powerful word you can use to begin a presentation is "YOU!" It is sheer dynamite! By comparison, all other words are firecrackers. The word "I" doesn't even pop.

Yet, what's the most common way speakers open up? They'll say, "I'm glad to be here." Then they'll eat up those first precious minutes talking trivia about themselves.

Use your first statement to draw your audience into the presentation and, if possible, start that statement with some form of the word *you.*

Humor is a great opener, but use it only if it relates specifically to your topic and only if your audience members can see themselves in it.

Make sure they understand that your speech is about them, not about you. Use *"I"* only when you are telling a very personal story; and keep those to a minimum.

Also, talk as if you are speaking to only one person. Always use the direct singular form: "YOU," not, "this group," or, "everyone in this audience." When you do speak to the group as a whole (and any time your statements could be construed as criticism), include yourself. Use pronouns like *we, us* and *our* to break down the "I/you" barrier.

Tactic #3: *Transcend cliches.* Amateurs all sound alike. They start with "I'm glad to be here," and end with "Thank you for listening to me." Their intent may be to sound gracious, but the audience hears such expressions as trite, worn out and impersonal cliches.

If a speaking engagement has special meaning to you, explain briefly why. If not, talk about something else your audience can identify with.

Declare war on all cliches and trite expressions and eliminate them from your speaking vocabulary. Develop your own openings, transitions and closings. Remember, your presentation should sound like it could only be made by you and that it would only fit the audience to which it's addressed.

Tactic #4: *Don't just stand there—do something.* 80% of what we get across to an audience is conveyed through our nonverbal messages. So, it's vital to think of your whole body as a communications medium

If possible, come out from behind the lectern and span the physical gulf between the podium and the audience. Get among the people and "press the flesh," as the politicians say. It works!

Also, don't just sway back and forth like you're trying to charm a cobra. Practice using carefully choreographed gestures and facial expressions until they become second nature to you, then adjust them to the size of your audience to make sure that everybody can see them.

Another good technique is to arrange for a "guinea pig" who will stand up when you ask for a volunteer. Your interaction with an individual or two can be fun for the audience and they'll identify with your volunteers. Just be careful not to embarrass or offend any person you are working with. The better your "guinea pig's" sense of humor and the more representative of the audience, the more mileage you will get out of this ploy.

Tactic #5: *Look your audience straight in the eyes, one person at a time.* Many novices either avoid eye contact altogether, or try to fake it by looking just above the heads of their audiences. The latter is better than the former, but neither involves the audience or builds credibility for you like constantly sweeping the room with your eyes and stopping periodically to fix on one person at a time. Of course, it's important to avoid the temptation to only connect with the eyes of a few people, or to give the impression you're only talking with one section of the group. Make eye contact with as many people as possible, and as often as possible, during your presentation.

Looking individuals in the eyes has a tremendous side benefit: it greatly reduces stage fright. The more contact you have with individuals, the more you get the feeling that you are talking to one or two persons. And, most of us feel much more comfortable with a few people than with a huge audience.

Tactic #6: *Answer their silent questions and objections.* A properly prepared presentation anticipates the questions and objections an audience has, and answers them. Also, by being sensitive to your audience, you can often tell from their expressions and body language what they are thinking.

If you can verbally express their reactions, and offer appropriate responses, you can do wonders to create the feeling of an on-going dialog. You might say something like: "If that's true, the logical question is . . ." or "Okay, it sounds good in theory, but how does it work in actual practice?" Then, you can go on to speak to their questions or concerns.

To avoid sounding condescending, don't overdo it. And, it often helps to preface your responses with affirming statements, like: "That's a fair enough question," or "We wondered the same thing . . . ."

The key to making the whole thing work is understanding your audience well enough to read them like a book.

Tactic #7: *Use verbal feedback.* Any time it's feasible, ask for verbal feedback from your audience, not just at the end, but throughout your presentation.

One good way to do that is to ask for a one-word or

short-phrase response, then wait for an answer. This works especially well when you have one key point you want to keep driving home.

For instance, during the ESE course, I say, "You cannot *not* communicate," because I think it's so vital to understand that. By the end of the first day, I can say the first two words and pause briefly. The entire group will finish my sentence. By the end of the second day, people will be paraphrasing the statement to each other, with things like: "You cannot not be successful." Then I know they have understood it and will remember it.

Whatever techniques you use to get verbal feedback from your audience, you can use to keep everyone involved.

Tactic #8: *Use nonverbal feedback.* Nonverbal signals are equally valuable in monitoring the reception of your audience. Nodding heads, receptive expressions, applause and other signals indicate your audience is with you.

Losing eye contact with individuals, collective shuffling of feet, movement of bodies, troubled expressions or guttural sounds are all signals that you are losing your audience.

If, at any point, you sense that your audience is losing interest or resisting what you are saying, stop and find out what the problem is. Then, do whatever it takes to regain attention and receptivity.

Sometimes, despite all your efforts to find out about your audience in advance, you will mis-read the group. If the reaction to what you are saying is pronounced enough, stop and ask what's going on.

For example, I will sometimes just come right out and say: "I sense that something doesn't fit, here . . . . Please tell me how you feel about what's going on." Usually, they will quickly reveal why they're reacting negatively, and I can shift gears and head in a more productive direction. I've never had an audience that didn't seem to appreciate that kind of sensitivity.

Tactic #9: *Gain acceptance of each crucial point before you move on to the next one.* This tactic is particularly helpful if people have to buy your support ideas before they will accept your main point or support your objective.

Many speakers, just like most salespeople, will ignore all kinds of signals that an audience is not buying the message. They get so caught up in their speech that they just keep plodding along in blissful ignorance. Then, when their speech is over, they can't understand why their audience didn't respond more positively.

I often use testing mechanisms to make sure my audience is buying my ideas. For instance, I'll ask something like: "Agreed?" or "Anybody have a problem with that?" Then I watch carefully to see how enthusiastically the majority of my audience responds. If they understand and buy my point, I move on to the next one.

If your style permits, that ploy can be even more powerful when it's used in a humorous way.

Tactic #10: *Always leave them begging for more.* No matter how many other good things you want to say, always quit before your audience is ready. If you have a time limit, stop a few minutes ahead of time. If no limit has been imposed, set your own.

Prepare a powerful and concise close. Then, at the slightest indication of waning interest, pull out your close and hit it with everything you've got. If they show signs that they want you to continue, **DON'T**. It's always better to leave them wanting more than to go out with a whimper.

Know when to say when.

Looking Ahead

We've talked about how to make an audience feel your personal presence and how to prepare to orchestrate the speaking process. And, in this chapter, we've focused on how to orchestrate your own personal style and amplify it for your audience.

In the next chapter, let's zero in on how to pull it all together and orchestrate your actual presentation for maximum impact.

CHAPTER SEVEN

HOW TO STAGE A DYNAMITE DELIVERY

> "I don't know anything about luck. I've never
> banked on it, and I'm afraid of people who do.
> Luck to me is something else: hard work and
> realizing what is opportunity and what isn't."
> —*Lucille Ball*

One of the things I enjoy most about living in California's Napa Valley is knowing and working very closely with some of the finest vintners in the world. It's a fascinating and rapidly changing business.

Like many industries, the vintners are facing intense competition. They are aggressively pursuing every opportunity in the global marketplace—especially the more than three million people who visit the valley each year and are potential long-term customers.

Winery executives, tour guides and salespeople are finding it necessary to put more impact into their presentations.

"It used to be that, if you made a good product, you expected to sell it, but that's not enough any more," says John Hawley, winemaker at Clos Du Bois Winery.

"Winery people are not often trained in speechmaking but end up doing it," he continues. He notes that lack of training and experience in any area can breed anxiety and ineffectiveness. "When you're comfortable, you're selling more, and that makes it a very worthwhile investment for the company."

Hundreds of winery owners, winemakers, executives and wine salespeople have participated in the ESE course, in customized speaking seminars and in private coaching, with the goal of equipping all key employees with confidence and speaking skills.

Gaining Confidence Through Control

Many executives are finding themselves in situations similar to the winery trade.

They're being called upon to stand up before groups and give important presentations, when they feel neither control, nor comfort, nor confidence. The purpose of this chapter is to show you how to gain control by orchestrating the whole speaking process.

Skilled wine masters readily see the connection between control and comfort. They tell me that scores of factors must be carefully controlled to produce a fine wine. Everything, from choosing the right grapes and harvesting them at precisely the right time to controlling a host of conditions in the delicate aging process, demands incredible attention to detail. A tiny mistake, anywhere along the perilous journey, can cost a winery millions of dollars.

Even though they readily admit there is an element of luck involved in producing an extraordinary wine, you can bet your last dollar they don't leave to chance anything they can control. The more carefully they prepare and guide the process, the better their chances of being able to cash in on luck when it happens.

It's precisely the same way in making presentations. The harder and smarter you work at it, the luckier you seem to get, and the more confident you feel about it.

In the preceding chapters, we've looked at a number of critical factors that need to be orchestrated individually for you to be in control of a presentation. Now, let's see how you can pull it all together into a symphonic presentation and turn your anxieties into positive, productive energy.

There are three elements you must control to be effective and confident.

Control Element #1: The External Environment

Experienced speakers know that physical facilities can have a big impact on how receptive an audience is, so they try to do everything they can to control the external environment.

If the room is too hot, for example, the people will feel drowsy and may nod off, no matter how good your presentation is. If it's too cold, they may get restless, and may even act hostile toward you.

Probably the biggest reason for problems with facilities is that no one takes responsibility for them. That means you have to. Even if you are at a hotel or other commercial facility, you can't always count on service personnel to make sure everything is right.

It's foolish to spend weeks preparing for a presentation, only have it shot down because the public address system doesn't work properly or because of some other trivial problem. And, it's never as effective to fix the blame as it is to ensure that a problem does not arise.

Again, planning is the key. Here's a common sense list of items that you should check before your presentation begins:

(1) *Comfortable temperature.* Make sure the thermostat is set right and that someone will monitor it while you are presenting.

(2) *Lighting.* Make sure it is bright enough to provide good eye contact without being uncomfortable. Also, if you'll need to be turning the lights up and down, appoint a reliable person to see about it.

(3) *Seating.* Provide reasonably comfortable chairs and arrange them so that you are the focal point and can easily maintain eye contact with everyone in the room.

(4) *Sound system.* Well before the meeting, check to see that it is adequate. If not, rent equipment if you have to, but make sure you can be heard. Also, make a last minute check to

assure that everything is working properly and that a competent person is available to make any needed adjustments.

(5) *Visual equipment*. Make sure everyone can see all visuals and that all equipment works properly. Provide for extra bulbs for projectors.

(6) *Distractions*. Try to remove or minimize any visual or auditory distractions. Post someone near a door to quiet any disturbances that may occur in hallways during your presentation.

What we're really talking about is hospitality—making your audience feel comfortable and important. People are impressed by attention to detail in matters of personal comfort and convenience.

So it's a good idea to think of yourself more as the host of a gathering than as a guest speaker. Good hosts always take care of details in advance so they can be free to focus all their attention on their guests.

Control Element #2: Control Yourself

The most crucial element to be controlled is yourself. Why? Because you are the message. The people in your audience will hear, understand and be moved by your content only to the extent that they experience the power of your personal presence. Your words will only have meaning when you give them meaning, your information will only be clear when you make it clear, your ideas will only have impact when you give them impact.

If you make your audience believe you, they will be more likely to believe your content. If you make them respond to you, they will respond to what you have to say. It doesn't work the other way around.

Your audience looks to you for clues to the value and importance of what you are saying. They look for those clues in your eyes, in your expressions, in your gestures and movements, they listen to the fervor and conviction in your voice, and they pick up and echo your energy level.

When you are in control of yourself, you exude confidence, credibility and energy. These three qualities come from your preparation, your comfort with yourself and your ability to turn anxiety into personal power.

Practice Makes Confidence

"Practice makes perfect," says the old saw; but I doubt it. I've certainly never made a perfect presentation, and I've never seen anyone else do it. But all of us can achieve excellence and a high level of confidence in our own abilities. That's what rehearsal does for you.

I recommend that you invest at least 10 hours in preparation for each hour you will be speaking, and at least 70% of that time should be spent in rehearsal. In other words, once you've thoroughly pre-planned your presentation, you've finished about 30% of your preparation. The remaining 70% involves getting *yourself* ready to deliver a credible and effective presentation.

Craig Williams, wine master at the Joseph Phelps Winery in Napa, California, is a real pro at what he does, and is often asked to speak about his work. Craig is by nature a rather quiet person with very controlled gestures. Someone once described him as "a man of measured words, careful in thought and deed."

"The idea of pre-planning the content and rehearsing, so the delivery will be more targeted, credible and clear, was like a light going off inside my head," he said.

After taking the ESE, Craig made a presentation to a large group, he was very anxious about doing well. So he carefully prepared: making notes on index cards, organizing the flow of ideas and rehearsing each part of his presentation.

"But when I got up to give my talk," he said, "wouldn't you just know it? I froze . . . . I started to sweat . . . I was under intense discomfort for about five minutes . . . it seemed like five hours."

"Finally, that light bulb went off again. I just turned my notes over and started talking to the audience," he said. "Since I knew the facts cold, it was easy. I just had to get unstuck from my written message."

What Craig had done was to so internalize the process of writing out and rehearsing his points that, when he got up in front of the group, the content was deeply ingrained in him. He had become his message.

The point is that you don't just read what you've prepared. You might glance at your notes to keep you on track. But, mostly, you speak from your heart and let what you know come out in a natural way. You simply tell your audience what you know and let your own feelings and energy show through. You are powerful stuff!

Get Real; Get Response

Maybe you've noticed, as I have, an odd thing about most amateur speakers. They are so afraid that somebody will think they are faking—that they won't come across as being real and natural—they end up looking and sounding like totally different people on stage.

I've seen people whose faces were lively and animated in conversations, but who looked like all the life had drained out of their faces when they got before a group. They might use dramatic and bold gestures, and move around like a boxer while they're talking one-on-one. But let them get in front of a group and they suddenly become so rigid you'd think they'd seen a ghost. Their hands might cling desperately to the lectern, or they might drop lifelessly to their sides, or they might clasp firmly in front of their private parts, like fig leaves.

The secret to coming across naturally in front of a group is to learn to amplify your own natural style. If you use gestures (and I hope you do), practice making them a little more pronounced. If you use vivid expressions (and I hope you do), practice making them a little more obvious and holding them a little longer so your audience can see them.

And, ask for a hand-held or lavaliere microphone so you can come out from behind the lectern and give people the full benefit of all your movements. If you plan to use a hand-held mike, use one in all your rehearsals and get so familiar with it that you can forget all about it while you are presenting.

If you use humor in private, use it when you speak. Your audience will love it. Don't try to be a comedian; very few people can pull it off. Stay away from jokes, unless you are a master at telling them. Just tell stories in a funny way and throw in humorous comments. Your goal is not to have your audience rolling in the aisles but merely to help them relax, enjoy themselves and get into what you are saying.

Also, remember that the mannerisms and expressions that make you interesting in private conversations will work when you are speaking to a group. Whatever you do to convey meaning in personal contacts, do more of it when you're in front of a group.

Don't Ever Let 'em See You Sweat

"It is not the same to talk of bulls as to be in the bullring," says an old Spanish proverb. But one thing an experienced matador will tell you is don't ever let the bull know you're afraid.

One of the most tell-tale signals that you are uncomfortable is to always be messing with yourself. Men tend to pull at their pants or belts, to keep straightening their ties, or to keep flipping their coats open and closed. Women seem to always be messing with their hair or make-up, or fumbling nervously for lost items in their purses.

The time to worry about the way you look is before you go on stage. I strongly recommend that speakers be very fussy about their personal appearance during their preparation. That means giving a great deal of care to choosing just the right clothes for the occasion and having them in perfect condition. It also means giving great care to such factors as shoes, accessories, manicure and hair styling.

When you walk into a room to speak, you should look like a million bucks, to be so confident in the way you look that you can forget all about your appearance.

Another thing that detracts considerably from your personal presence and poise is unnecessary movements. Shifting or swaying back and forth, fumbling with papers or glasses or any purposeless motion makes your audience uncomfortable and identifies you as a sweating amateur.

The way you handle your mistakes in front of a group can also have a big impact on the way your audience perceives you. Don't let mistakes rattle you, and never admit to a goof. If it is so obvious that you have to acknowledge it, make a quick joke out of it and go on. Otherwise, ignore it and go right on. If you forget a line, or leave out a whole point, the audience won't even notice it unless you confess it.

The best way to make the audience relax and get into what you have to say is for you to relax and get into it. And, the best way to do that is to be so prepared and practiced that you know you can handle anything.

A strange thing happens when you act confident; it actually makes you feel confident. And, when you feel confident, you can infuse your presentation with all the energy that would otherwise be bled off by anxiety. You can come alive, and make your audience come alive.

Redirect The Nervous Energy

"It's hard to feel confident when my knees keep knocking together," one participant in our course told me.

Most people feel a case of the jitters just before a performance. For some people, it becomes an immobilizing fear.

- Willard Scott, NBC's happy-go-lucky weatherman once confessed in an interview that in the early stages of his career he became so frozen by stage fright that he had to drop out of broadcasting until he conquered it.

- Gloria Steinem, a well-known women's leader, said in her autobiography that she went through times in the early stages of her career when she would become violently sick in the hours before she was to make a speech.

- Henry Fonda, the ever-popular and laid-back actor, reportedly became so anxious before each of his more than 150 performances in the stage version of "Mr. Roberts" that he often feared he would not be able to go on.

- And, John F. Kennedy reportedly held one hand behind him during his entire Democratic presidential nomination acceptance speech because, while waiting to go on stage, he had chewed his fingernails off so badly that his hand was bleeding.

So, if you get the jitters about standing in front of a group you are in good company. But don't let it hold you back, just as all the above people didn't let it stop them.

Actually, some tension before you speak can be very positive. It gets your adrenalin flowing, stimulates your pulse rate and creates a tremendous amount of energy that you can use to advantage.

Here are some simple but highly effective techniques which can enable you to redirect all that tension into the creative energy and enthusiasm you need to stage a powerful performance.

(1) *Control your breathing.* Slow down your breathing and consciously take deeper breaths—from the diaphragm instead of the upper chest. The action redirects your attention and the increased oxygen to your brain triggers a physical relaxation response.

(2) *Yawn.* Of course, you don't want to do this in front of an audience. But yawn as many times as you can before you go

to the meeting. It's very difficult to yawn and be tense at the same time.

(3) *Laugh a little*. Even a nervous little laugh to yourself helps to relieve tension. Light-hearted banter with other people before you go on stage will help you relax and it will make you feel more at home with the group.

(4) *Tense up all your muscles, then let them go*. If you are subtle about it, you can tense up and let go several times in your chair, without anyone in your audience seeing it. The feeling of relaxing is almost euphoric.

(5) *Drink warm water*. Ice water constricts your pipes and makes your voice sound squeaky, but room-temperature water helps to relax your throat and neck muscles.

(6) *Rearrange the furniture*. Just a little. Shift the props around, move the lectern or adjust the chairs. The movement helps you relax and the physical rearranging helps you to feel in control.

(7) *Do some simple, positive visualization*. Form a mental picture of yourself standing before the audience, performing smoothly and powerfully, and imagine the people responding with great enthusiasm. It's the same technique Olympic athletes use to "see themselves through" their performances. Don't picture failure; visualize success.

(8) *Use positive self-talk*. Psyche yourself *up*, not *out*. Instead of saying, "Oh, God, how did I get myself into this?" try, "I'm ready. I feel good about this. I feel confident." Your subconscious will believe what it hears most. So make sure it hears positive self-talk.

Always remember that you are much harder on yourself than almost anyone in your audience will be. They will be much less concerned about how well you do than about how they experience your presentation. Often, their worst thought will be, "I'm glad it's you up there, and not me!"

You Can Control Yourself

There are many things we cannot control: the weather, events that happen around us, or even poor planning and execution by the people who invite us to speak.

But we can control ourselves: our actions, our expressions, our gestures, our voices, the way we walk in—all the things that really matter.

Most of all, we can control our emotions instead of letting them run away with us.

In making thousands of speeches and presentations, one thing I've noticed is that the more attention I give to the things I can control, the less I have time to worry about those things which are beyond my control.

Control Element #3: Your Audience

The first two minutes you're before an audience can make or break any presentation. And, the first 20 seconds are nothing short of critical. It's where you capture their attention and set the stage for your whole presentation.

Yet how many times have you seen this scenario? A speaker stands up and cracks a few jokes to warm up the audience. Then, abruptly, the mood changes drastically. The smile disappears, the eyes drop to the lectern and the monotonous reading begins. It's like saying, "Okay! Fun's over! Time to get down to business!" Or maybe the speaker doesn't even bother to warm up the audience.

Hey! Speaking is a lot like making love. You start with a little romance, you get comfortable with each other and you build a little confidence. You look deeply into each other's eyes, you get to know each other, you tune in to each other's thoughts and feelings. When you both know it's right, well

. . . you know what I'm talking about.

I'm not suggesting you get amorous with your audiences, but I do wish to imply emphatically that building a relationship between presenter and audience requires tact, warmth, diplomacy and confidence.

Take Charge Immediately

Usually, the toughest part of making a speech is getting started, yet it's also the most crucial part.

One reason it's so hard to get started is that there is a psychological law of inertia at work in the beginning. You know, a body at rest tends to remain at rest and a body in motion tends to remain in motion at the same speed and in the same direction unless acted upon by an outside force.

Frankly, most business meetings are so poorly run that the audience is almost always "at rest" when we stand up to speak. Guess who has to act as the outside force to get an audience moving at the right speed and in the right direction—YOU. Nothing productive happens until you make it happen.

There are two equally vital tactics you can use to take charge immediately.

The first is what I call owning the environment. That means you show by your appearance and actions that you are ready to take charge. The way you do that is a little hard to describe but it has to do with your air of confidence, the look in your eyes and the expression on your face, the way you walk to the podium, your entire demeanor. It's the quality that causes people to immediately stop what they are doing and pay attention when certain people walk into a room.

Perhaps the best way to explain it is to talk about its opposite. Haven't you noticed how some people seem to be worn by their clothes instead of wearing them, how they seem to be tentative and uncertain about everything they do and say. That's the opposite of owning one's environment.

Speakers fail to own their environment when they do things like thumping the mike to see if it's working, or fumbling through their notes trying to find a starting place, or telling how unqualified they are to speak on the subject.

Owning your environment is making everything about you say, "I'm important, you are important, we have something important and exciting to do together, so let's get on with it!" When you can do that, you can take charge immediately.

The second tactic for taking charge is to do or say something to command attention. Notice that I said *command* attention, not *demand* attention. You can command attention in soft ways, in funny ways, in dramatic ways— whatever best suits your style and the occasion.

The key to making it work is to get the audience involved as fully and as quickly as possible.

One good technique is to get the audience to do something with you. It can be a fun activity or an exercise designed to help focus the topic.

Another effective technique is to do something verbal: ask a startling question or make a startling statement, tell a compelling or funny story, or to simply tell why the topic should matter to the audience.

You've done your homework, your audience is waiting to see what you're going to do, so get the ball rolling quickly and effectively.

Stay One Step Ahead Of Your Audience

If you get caught up in what you have to say and your audience doesn't, you've got big troubles. Constantly read their response and make whatever adjustments are required to stay in charge.

Whatever you do, don't let some individual or group within the audience get away with drawing attention from you to themselves.

One of the toughest audiences I ever spoke to was the annual meeting of a group of building supply salespeople.

They always looked upon that occasion as a time to have a good time, which was okay. But they went beyond having fun. They were being rowdy and yelling at each other up until the time I was introduced. When I stood to speak, they kept right on shouting at each other, laughing gustily and generally being disruptive.

As a professional speaker, I had no intention of letting them wrestle the session away from me. So I started pausing every time a group of them would start talking to each other. I would just stand quietly until some of the people around them started signaling for them to get quiet. Before long, they would get the message.

Within a few minutes, peer pressure had forced them to calm down. Eventually, most of them began to listen and some got pretty involved in what I was saying. I wouldn't call it a great presentation, but it stands out in my memory as one in which I averted a major disaster.

Of course, the reason that was such a memorable experience for me was its rarity. Most audiences are very courteous and cooperative.

For the skilled speaker, however, courtesy and co-operation are not enough. You want them to be interested, involved and perhaps even enthusiastic in their response. To get that kind of response you need to be responsive to them. If you sense that what you are doing is not getting through, shift gears and go in a different direction.

Bring Plenty Of Ammunition

That's why it's important to bring plenty of extra ammunition with you. It doesn't mean you have to throw out your planned presentation; just change your methods.

If, for instance, the audience is not involved when you ask questions and answer them yourself, you might try asking questions and waiting for the group to answer. If statistics don't turn them on but stories do, pull out a few extra stories. If the audience is questioning your facts, back them up with more support data.

Gerry Kenny, the bridge and tunnel builder we talked about earlier, told me about an interesting technique he uses to stay one jump ahead of his audience. Gerry uses quite a few slides in his presentations and he noticed that some people were paying more attention to the slides than to him. To counter that, he started moving around the room and speaking from different locations. They would never know where his voice would come from next, so they had to keep their minds on him, just to keep up with him.

The important thing is to learn how to think on your feet and always stay ahead of your audience. That's where your extensive research comes in; it gives you plenty of options you can pursue.

Go For Response

Perhaps the most important thing to keep in mind as you seek to control your audience is the response you want to get from them—your objective for making the presentation.

If they are not with you after you've made your first or second major point, they're not likely to be with you when you come to the end. So it's crucial to keep getting their commitment on each point as you go along. Someone called it getting "the commitment on the conviction."

Also, don't look at the closing as nothing more than a way to end your presentation. Relate to it as if you are closing a sale. Get them to do something, if it's nothing more than to nod their heads in agreement.

Remember, the bottom line is always the bottom line. You only succeed to the degree that your audience gives you the precise response you want.

Looking Ahead

"I love it when a good plan comes together," actor George Peppard used to tell his gutsy team after they'd pulled off a nearly impossible feat each week on "The A-Team" television series.

And, that's exactly what happens when an effective and productive presentation is given—someone (or perhaps several people) makes a good plan come together.

Good presentations don't just happen, no matter how many you've done. They are always the result of careful planning and skillful execution, or what I like to think of as orchestration.

In our next chapter, let's explore what makes a memorable presentation.

CHAPTER EIGHT

HOW TO BOOST IMPACT AND RETENTION

> "Everything should be made as simple
> as possible, but no simpler."
> —*Albert Einstein*

Executives and other experts often get frustrated because an audience doesn't grasp in a one-hour speech what they have spent a lifetime learning. They want audiences and co-workers to understand quickly, to believe totally and respond enthusiastically. Too often, it just doesn't happen.

Part of the problem is the sheer complexity of our world these days. There is so much going on in so many areas that affect us, and conditions change so rapidly that we simply cannot keep up with it all. As scientific futurist Daniel A. Burrus often says, "If it works, it's obsolete."

What we all tend to do is grab a little corner of the world that we can comprehend, and become specialists in that area. So, more and more we find ourselves speaking to other people who may be specialists at what they do but generalists at what we are trying to explain.

I often work with companies whose research and development departments are not able to communicate with the sales and marketing departments, where financial officers can't get through to production managers, and where nobody seems to be able to communicate with customers.

People in different disciplines speak different languages. They have different ways of thinking and acting, and no frame of reference for understanding each other. At the same time, we are all becoming increasingly dependent upon each other for survival and productivity. Therefore, performance and profitability suffer at all levels. As we dash madly toward the twenty-first century, that problem will continue to grow more acute.

We all have a compelling need to find better ways to have our messages heard, understood, believed, remembered and acted upon. This chapter is designed to enable you to boost the impact of everything you say and to make it more memorable.

Audiences Need All The Help They Can Get

Start with the assumption that what you know so well, others don't know at all. It is not at all condescending for you to assume the role of teacher and, in many cases, coach. You only become condescending when you act as if what you know makes you superior to those you would teach.

Actually, the very expertise that makes you effective at what you do can create barriers between you and those you would teach. It's not as if you can bore a hole in someone's head, insert a funnel and pour all your knowledge and conviction into them.

To be effective as a presenter, you have to meet people where they are, get them excited enough to mentally and emotionally give you their hands, then lead them to where you want them to be.

It might be helpful to think of yourself as a tour guide, leading people around inside your mind and heart, showing and explaining to them the intimate details of your own turf. Bear in mind that they will always compare and relate what you show them to the details of their own turfs (where they are the experts) and to what they have seen and experienced of other turfs.

That means their abilities and willingness to grasp your ideas fully are limited by their own perceptions of reality. It takes a great deal of love, concern and skill to get people to embrace your own perceptions of reality.

Rebuilding Joe

My very first one-on-one coaching experience with a video camera was also one of the toughest challenges I've ever faced.

Thank God for people who believe in us. Arthur Friedman, head of Nalco Chemical Company in Oakbrook, Illinois, believed in me. Although I had left Dale Carnegie and had started out on my own, I had not dreamed of becoming a speaking coach. But Art thought I had what it took and invited me in to provide private coaching for one of his top scientists, whom I will refer to as Joe (not his real name).

In his field, Joe was outstanding but inept as a communicator. He simply could not get his ideas across in presentations or even in talking with individuals.

Joe stammered and had another speech problem which made his enunciation sound garbled. Physically, he presented himself very poorly. He was untidy, his hair flopped down in his face, he had dandruff and he sweated profusely. He also wore ill-fitting, out of style clothes and very unattractive glasses, which he kept pushing back up on his head. He had terrible eye contact with his audience. In short, he was a mess.

Add to this heaping bad news, he was very suspicious. He didn't trust anybody.

Art felt I could work with Joe because he had developed some trust for me earlier, when I was his instructor in the Dale Carnegie course. And, Art had a pressing need for Joe to become more effective in communicating. So the timing was right.

It turned out to be a glorious success for all three of us. Joe worked hard and became good at making his highly technical presentations and in his personal communication. Art told me later that I had billed the company way too little. It was a real emotional and professional growth step for me to work with and see the transformation of Joe.

Bridging The Gap

What emerged in me during those coaching sessions with Joe was an awareness that in all forms of communication, especially speaking, we need to lure our audience across the bridge from where they are to where we want them to be.

Let me share with you a few of the techniques I've learned to use in getting my points across more emphatically and having them remembered. These work in virtually all forms of communication, but especially in speaking and making formal presentations.

Technique #1: Clarify Your Meanings

The same words often have different meanings to different people. To give you an idea of just how confusing it can be, Benjamin Franklin once compiled a list of 214 synonyms (all in English) for the word *drunk*, and each of them has a slightly different shading of meaning. The 500 most commonly used words in our language have a combined total of more than 14,000 meanings. When you add to this the fact that we can completely change the meanings of words by the nonverbal signals we mix with them, you can see how confusing words can get.

Clarifying your terms is simply making it clear what your words and expressions mean to you, then testing to see that people in your audience understand those meanings.

How can you do that? The most direct way is to start your presentation with a definition of the key terms you will be using. Another direct way is to stop and define new terms as they come up. Those methods are useful when you are dealing with technical information with an audience which is rather unsophisticated in that technical area. But they seem rather stilted, and may sound condescending, in other speaking situations.

What I most often use is a more indirect approach. You may have noticed that, throughout this book, I've used expressions like "in other words," and "simply stated," and "what we're really talking about is . . . ." That is neither an attempt to be wordy nor careless redundancy. Those expressions are vehicles I use to further clarify points I am making. In other words, I will often state an idea one way, then come back and state it a little differently using a phrase to set it up.

One caution: don't overuse one phrase. Some people grab a phrase like "you know," and repeat it so often you can bet there is always a high probability that their next sentence will begin with "you know." When that happens, we are not clarifying our meanings, we are habitually using a trite expression to buy a little time to think up something to say. In addition, we're parading before our audience how nervous we are. Don't sound like a broken record; use variety in your introductory phrases.

Another excellent way to clarify your meaning is to use examples, or analogies, or illustrative stories. I often use the term "for instance" to illustrate my point. I do it even more when I speak because people can't jump back and read a spoken sentence that was confusing to them. It also helps people to make a connection between my illustrations and my points. Again, mix it up with expressions like "for example," and "for instance," and "let me illustrate."

Testing to make sure people have understood involves asking questions that cause people to feed back to you their interpretations of what you have just said.

Now, getting feedback involves more than simply asking, "Did you get that?" A question like that implies that you are testing their ability to comprehend. Asked often enough, it could create the impression that you think they are dumb. Instead, use an approach like this: "I'm not sure I made that very clear . . . what did you understand me to say?"

Of course, that tactic works much better with small groups, and even then should be used sparingly. Overused, it could create the impression that you don't know what you are talking about. Use it only on meanings that are critical to the understanding of your basic message.

However you do it, always make sure that people understood you to say what you meant to say.

Technique #2: Use Symbols

I'm sure you've heard the old expression, "We're talking about apples and oranges." That's a widely understood metaphor which means, "We're using similar words but talking about something quite different." And, it sets up beautifully what I want to say.

Idiomatic expressions, metaphors, similes and other symbols are great aids to understanding, but only if they mean the same things to your audience that they mean to you.

For example, you may say to an audience, "We're really going out on a limb," and you may mean you're taking a chance. But, if your audience is made up of Shirley MacLaine fans, they may interpret the expression to mean that you are getting into metaphysics.

A more common mistake is to use a symbol that has no meaning at all to your audience. Technical acronyms and symbols that are bantered about by the experts in your discipline can only confuse a non-technical audience.

I highly recommend that you use symbols; they can enable people to grasp quickly even the most complex ideas and information. But always make sure those symbols have meaning to your audience.

Technique #3: Guide Your Audience With Transitions

One of the toughest challenges in listening to a speech is to understand how ideas and bits of information relate to each other. To an audience, it may seem that you are talking about one thing, then you suddenly shift to another subject.

Remember, you understand the relationships of your ideas and information, and you have had the benefit of organizing your material on paper, perhaps even on charts or diagrams. Your audience is probably hearing ideas for the first time. They may feel as if they are swimming around in a sea of words.

Transitions are handles people use to pull bits of information and ideas together. Always take great care to give your audience plenty of handles they can use to connect your points.

Some of the transitional statements I've found most useful are:

- "We've seen how . . . now, let's focus on . . . ."
- "Let's have a look at . . . ."
- "Moving on to . . . ."
- "Turning now to . . . "
- "Which raises the logical question . . . ."
- "If that's true, then . . . ."
- "Right now, you're probably wondering . . . ."
- "We've seen the big picture, now let's look at some of the details of . . . ."
- "Looking at it another way . . . ."

My purpose here is not to give you an exhaustive list of transitional statements to memorize, but to show you how they work. Choose statements that sound natural for you and customize them to your audience.

Think of transitions as signs you are giving your audience to guide them through unfamiliar territory. They will appreciate them.

Technique #4: Oversimplify and Repeat

People are bombarded with so many messages these days

that our only hope of having our ideas heard and remembered is to oversimplify our messages and repeat them again and again.

That approach may seem offensive to you if you are an expert in some technical field. Doctors, engineers and scientists, for example, often feel that oversimplifying complex ideas will weaken them, or maybe even destroy their integrity.

Remember, your objective is not to impress people with how much you know, but to explain what they need to know in order to do what you want them to do. Therefore, the most relevant question is always, "What do they need to know and understand to give me the response I want?"

Your challenge, as an expert, is to reduce every idea to a simple explanation that anyone in your audience can grasp and remember, then to repeat it often enough that they cannot forget it.

Probably the best way to see how the technique of oversimplification and repetition works is to watch and analyze network television commercials. The advertising agencies which produce them are masters at the art. A line like "Trust your memories to Kodak," repeated again and again, will be remembered for years.

Always make it a point to encapsulate each of your main points in a very simple and memorable sentence and keep hammering away at it. Of course, you don't want to sound like you are saying the same thing over and over, so you have to use a little imagination in the way you do it.

Summaries provide one excellent device for repetition. When you finish your first point, state it again before you move on. Then, repeat your first two points before you move on to the third one. As you get ready to close your speech, repeat all the main points. Your audience may not remember all the support information you gave, but they are much more likely to leave with the main points fixed firmly in their minds—if the points are simple enough, and if you have repeated them often enough.

Technique #5: Use Handouts

One of the greatest hindrances to emotional impact, understanding and retention is taking excessive notes.

What often happens is that, if a speaker is good, people in the audience will often want to make sure they can remember certain ideas, so they write furiously throughout the whole presentation. That poses several problems.

First, it forces the note-takers to keep everything on an intellectual level. They get so caught up in writing down the words that they are insulated from the emotional impact the speaker intended.

Second, the ideas flow through their heads, into their arms and onto the paper, often without being processed. The plan seems to be to get all the ideas down, so none will escape, then to try to understand them later. Which brings up the next problem.

Third, most people who take voluminous notes either file them away or put them into a massive stack of other notes and never get around to reviewing them.

The net result is that people don't feel, comprehend or remember what they've heard, no matter how good their intentions might have been. If you've ever spoken to such an audience, you know that it can feel like you're talking to a room full of dictating machines—all of which are connected to paper shredders.

For this reason, I try to use handouts as often as possible. I will preface my presentation with a statement like: "You don't need to worry about taking notes . . . . I've put everything important that I'm going to say today into a handout, which I'll give you when I've finished . . . . So, please, put away your pens and let's enjoy this time together."

I strongly recommend that you use handouts. However, there are some pitfalls to avoid.

(1) Don't make them too detailed: people won't read long handouts. Keep them short, simple and highly customized

(2) Don't give them out at the beginning: people will bury their heads in the handouts and ignore the critical first few minutes of your speech. Announce that you'll give them out later, then go right into your presentation. Note: It might be necessary to give them out in advance if you are presenting technical information and having them fill in blanks. If so, prepare them in a way that no one can figure out what to write in until you tell them.

(3) Don't just hand out papers indiscriminately or people won't value any of them. Treat each handout as if it has great value. Romance it, talk about how vital the information it contains is, and count out the exact number you need for everyone to have one. Never leave extra copies lying around the room.

One side benefit to having a sharp, two or three page handout is that people will often share it with others when they ask what you spoke about. That spreads your ideas and information around to a broader audience, and using the handout as a reporting guide reinforces what you said in the mind of the person who heard you speak.

Handouts can be a great aid in boosting your impact and enabling people to remember what you have said.

Technique #6: Move Beyond Words to Experience

There's a wise old saying that goes something like this:

> "What I hear, I forget;
> What I see, I remember;
> What I experience, I become."

I love to speak to large audiences about public speaking, and I enjoy writing about it. But neither of those activities creates the high level sense of reward that comes from working with a group of a dozen people in the Executive Speaking Experience, a customized seminar or in one-on-

one coaching. Why? Because I find myself crying and laughing at the same time when I see the tremendous growth that happens when people actually experience for themselves the techniques that I teach.

You can't always get that involved with your audiences, nor can I. But the more we can enable people to experience for themselves, the higher the quality of learning will be.

Think about your own subject matter and the audiences you work with. Is there some way you can enable them to experience your ideas for themselves? Can you get them to do something that enables them to make discoveries about your information and apply it to their own lives?

Real estate salespeople tell me that prospects won't physically buy a house until they take psychological ownership of it. They have to mentally see themselves moving in and turning it into their own home before they will sign on the dotted line.

That's a good goal to keep in mind any time you try to communicate with any audience—enable them to take psychological ownership of the ideas and information. If you can get them to do that, through whatever experiencing process you devise, you can be sure that what you say will have more impact and that it will be long remembered.

Looking Ahead

Amateur speakers see themselves as spouting out ideas and information and believe it is up to their audiences to sort through them and remember what's important. Then, they get frustrated because it doesn't happen.

Skilled speakers assume full responsibility for getting their messages across clearly, for having as much impact as possible on their audiences and for assisting those who hear them in remembering the most important ideas.

Now, in the next chapter, let's turn our attention to one of the most powerful vehicles for helping people understand, remember and act.

CHAPTER NINE

ADD IMPACT THROUGH VISUALS

"A picture is worth a thousand words."
—Ancient oriental proverb

All you need to do is to look around you to see that our culture has become very visual in its orientation and expectations.

- Some 99% of all American homes have at least one television set and more than two-thirds have two.

- Many offices, conference rooms and showrooms feature videotape and videodisk players.

- Computer terminals and personal computers—many with color monitors, have become regular fixtures on offices desks.

- Magazines, catalogs and brochures now flood our homes and offices with vivid and colorful pictures.

- Huge billboards line our highways and elaborate signs direct us to business establishments.

- With the coming of holographic imaging, fiber-optic and satellite communications hookups and video conferences, visual impact will soon become the name of the communications game.

What it means is that people have increasingly become attuned to seeing as well as hearing every message. And, speakers who rely totally on oral presentations now have to compete with all the visual impact and stimulation. That's the bad news.

The good news is that creating and using powerful and effective visuals is much less a hassle than it once was. In the past, you either had to be an artist or hire an artist to make good graphics or even simple charts and diagrams. Now, with all the equipment and computer software available, even rank amateurs can create impressive graphics— quickly, simply and effectively.

What's more, skillfully executed visuals can make a routine presentation come alive. If you know how to use them, visuals can greatly enhance your presentation. But, if they get out of hand, they can quickly turn a highly professional speech into an amateurish nightmare.

This chapter won't make you an expert, but it can help you understand the basics of how to add visual impact to all your presentations.

Why Use Visuals?

Most of us use visuals all day every day. We point to something we want people to notice, we show pictures to clarify our meanings and we may even draw crude sketches to illustrate our ideas or instructions.

If you stop and think about it, we can use visuals in exactly those same ways when we are making a structured presentation.

Here are some specific ways you can use visuals:

(1) *Use visuals to boost audience interest.* People are attracted to what catches their eye. Visuals are especially effective when you have to cover a lot of details that might otherwise get boring and tedious.

(2) *Use visuals to simplify and clarify.* Complex issues and explanations can often be greatly simplified with the use of visuals.

(3) *Use visuals to make abstract ideas concrete.* Visuals can add a sensory dimension to your words. If, for instance, you are describing a new building or product you're going to create, some in the audience might have great difficulty visualizing it. Everybody is certain to imagine it differently. An artist's conception can make your explanation tangible.

(4) *Use visuals to increase your efficiency.* If you've got to cover an hour's presentation in five minutes, you can greatly increase the speed of getting your message across by using visuals. Instead of explaining statistics, numbers and other data, you can show them instantly on graphs or charts.

(5) *Use visuals to show relationships.* If you are trying to explain to a group of employees how they fit into the big picture, you can quickly make it clear with a structural chart. Comparisons of statistical data are much easier to explain with bar charts, graphs or pie charts. You can also use visuals to show how the major points of your presentation fit together.

(6) *Use visuals to emphasize.* A bold, colorful visual can call attention to—and reinforce—your important points

(7) *Use visuals to strengthen retention.* By using visuals to summarize and review all major points, you give people an image to hold forever in their minds.

As you can see, there are a variety of ways you can use visuals. The important thing is to make sure that you know what you want to accomplish with each of them and how to create the right visual for each purpose.

Visuals That Work Best

You have a wide range of visual options to choose from. But one of the keys to making them work for you is to choose the most effective tool for each objective.

Here are only a few of the tools you have available, and some ideas on how they can be most useful to you.

(1) *Overhead transparencies*. These are effective with small to medium sized audiences especially when you have a lot of information to cover. They are easy to prepare and you can change them at the last minute. You can also get them commercially prepared in color, quickly and inexpensively. Avoid the temptations to overload them and to use too many of them.

(2) *Slides*. Slides enable you to project graphs, photographs, illustrations, mood-setting patterns, build-up sequences, charts and special effects. They are much better in quality than overheads and can be sequenced to eliminate the hassle of shuffling them around. Professionally prepared title slides can be expensive. Use them when you need to make a first-class impression, or when you are giving the same presentation a number of times. You'll also need a darker room for them than for transparencies, so it's a good idea to show only a few during a presentation.

(3) *Movie films*. If you want to show anything in motion or operation, film or video is your best bet. A short, well-made movie can get people fully involved in what you are saying. Be prepared to pay considerably more if you go with film.

(4) *Videotape*. Videotape offers some advantages over film, but it also has disadvantages. Since it can be played back instantly, activities can be shown quickly and presentations can be prepared at the last-minute. Videotapes are easily portable, but (at least for the present) screen size limits the use of video to small or medium size groups.

(5) *Posters and display boards*. These don't require darkened rooms. They can be prepared by hand but it can be time-consuming and requires some artistic skill. If you need

changeability, you can use magnetic or Velcro boards where you can mount or dismount objects at will.

(6) *Flip charts and chalk boards.* These two old standbys work well in informal presentations and don't require a darkened room. They are highly flexible and adaptable, and are great for audience involvement. But they can be messy and time consuming. You can reduce the messiness and amount of time consumed by preparing—either partially or completely—flip charts in advance. The key to making them work is customization.

(7) *Multi-media.* This simply means using a combination of visual and/or audio tools, and can be very effective. Slides with a sound track, a group of slide projectors working in a pre-arranged sequence, or a combination of slide projectors, movie film and audio track can provide powerful impact, especially in a large auditorium. Of course, these systems take considerable time and expertise to prepare and operate, and cost can be considerable. But, if you need maximum impact, nothing else comes close to the sheer power of a well-designed and flawlessly executed multi-media show.

Many excellent tools are available to help you add impact to your presentation. What's important is not how many you use, but that you choose precisely the right ones for your objectives and your audience.

Using Visual Aids Effectively

There is an art to using visuals, and the more experience you have with them the easier it will become. But here are some tips that can make your visuals come alive, even if you've never used this valuable aid before.

(1) *Think of visuals only as aids.* Remember, you are the message; if your visuals are overpowering, there's no reason

for you to be there. Use your visuals only as supports, not as crutches.

(2) *Each visual should help you make a point.* Visuals are there to emphasize. Never throw in a visual just because it's attractive or impressive. If it doesn't help you make a point, don't use it.

(3) *Make only one point with each visual.* Several messages on one graphic can confuse your audience and take away from the impact of all your visuals.

(4) *Keep all visuals simple.* A visual is designed to give a message in only a few seconds. If it has to stay on a screen longer than 10 seconds, it will become boring. Be sure the visual is not complex or complicated. Your audience should be able to recognize your message immediately.

(5) *Start with a general idea and move to the specific.* Well-designed visuals can help people to see the big picture before you plunge into more detailed information. That way, they won't be lost in a fog as you move from one point to the next.

(6) *Show comparisons, examples or analogies.* Often, you can explain complex ideas by graphically showing how they fit with what the audience already knows.

(7) *Make your visual material real and natural.* If you have something real such as pictures, sketches and cartoons, people can sometimes "see the picture" almost immediately and grasp the abstract concepts they represent. In any case, make sure your audience doesn't have trouble interpreting the symbols you use on your visuals.

(8) *Use the visual format that best portrays your message.* Statistical data, technical information and complex relationships can often be simplified by using tables, graphs, pie charts and bar charts. Choose the one that will work best for

your information. Consult a commercial artist if you need help.

(9) *Build in continuity.* A well-coordinated set of visuals is like a well-designed room—it looks finished and professional. Stick to one type style and size, one format and one color combination.

(10) *Use action and vivid colors in titles.* Active nouns and verbs make your message catchy and get it across much more easily than passive ones. And color adds impact to visuals by highlighting and creating moods and emotions. Try to make your visuals fun to watch.

With these simple guidelines, you can create visuals that will add a lot of punch to any presentation.

Blending Visuals With Oral Presentation

Ideally, visuals work synergistically with your oral presentation to create a greater impact than either could produce alone. Therefore, your visual aids must be tied very closely to the material you will be presenting orally.

You can blend your text and visual aids in a variety of ways.

(1) *Let your visuals grow out of your text, not vice versa.* Visuals work best when they illuminate the text instead of being used as a crutch. Although visuals often take considerable time to prepare (especially if you're having them professionally prepared), it is better to start your planning early enough to have your text refined before you block out your visuals. Committing your visuals first can lock you into a flow of ideas that may not be the best approach—maybe even box you into a presentation that won't work. Always develop your text, then prepare your visuals.

(2) *Use visual aids for the transitions of your speech.* Well-designed visuals can enable the audience to see how the information all hangs together. For example, build-up title slides or transparencies can be used to show where each new bit of information fits with what has gone before.

(3) *Keep all aids out of sight until you are ready to use them, then put them aside when you've finished.* If your audience can see visuals before you are ready to talk about them, you could find yourself competing with your own reinforcements. People are drawn to visuals and will be busy trying to see or read them rather than listening to you. So always make sure no one can see your visuals until you are ready to use them. Once you've finished with them, quickly put them out of sight.

(4) *Talk to your audience, not to your visuals.* Avoid the temptation to look at your visuals while you are talking about them. That will help you maintain contact with your audience. Talking to your visuals makes you fade into the background and puts the visuals center stage. Get so familiar with each visual that you can tell with a quick glance what point it illustrates, then immediately resume eye contact with your audience. Your audience must always be your primary target, not your visuals.

(5) *Introduce your illustrations in the text but don't read wording on visuals.* Audience members should never be left wondering, even for a few seconds, why a particular visual is being displayed. A quick oral reference to the visual will help your audience understand why you are using that particular aid. That's why it's so crucial to practice your timing. To have impact, each visual must come up at precisely the instant you make a reference to it and must be removed the instant you are through with it.

(6) *Make visuals clearly visible, but don't let them block you out.* Few things are more frustrating to an audience than to

have to sit through a presentation without being able to see the visual aids. Put them up high enough that everyone in the room can see them without having to stretch their necks or get up and move around. Also, be careful to avoid getting behind your visuals. It is imperative that you maintain eye contact at all times with your audience, if at all possible.

(7) *Be sensitive to audience reaction.* Watch for nonverbal signals that people are not correctly interpreting or understanding your visuals, or that they are reacting negatively to them. Visuals may be very clear to you, because you prepared them, but they may not be so readily understandable to your audience. If you sense the audience is not grasping visual messages, slow down and explain them a little more fully. Also, if you are using slides and have the room darkened, watch for signs that your audience is getting drowsy. Some people have conditioned themselves to fall asleep any time they are in a darkened room. If you sense that people are getting drowsy, turn up the lights and do something to awaken everybody.

(8) *Avoid spending too much time on any one visual.* Television programs have geared people to expect constant motion and a complete change of scenery every five or six seconds. Most visuals are still. If you add extremely long exposure time, you are setting the stage for boredom and restlessness in your audience. Ten seconds is maximum for effective exposure on most visuals. If the nature of your material calls for very complex visuals that take longer to cover, do *something* to break the monotony. If you are using an overhead projector, you might cover most of the transparency and reveal one part at a time, or you might cover the entire transparency with a black sheet and keep uncovering it when you need to refer to it. Another tactic you can use with transparencies or slides is to use an electronic arrow to point to various parts of the visual as you talk about it. Come up with some way to create a feeling of change and motion. But, whatever you do, don't let the

projector flash a sudden white light on the screen. A bright light in a darkened room is like a slap in the face.

(9) *Arrange all visuals for quick and easy access.* Nothing detracts more from the professional quality of a presentation than having the speaker fumble with transparencies or slides that have gotten out of sequence or are turned the wrong way. When that happens, it not only irritates the audience and makes you look bad, it causes your confidence level to drop to zero. Always make sure your visuals are arranged properly, that they are secure enough that they won't fall, and that you can get to them quickly and easily.

(10) *Practice using your visuals until you can do it smoothly, without even having to think about what you are doing.* Properly executed, the operation of your visuals is almost unnoticed. You move through them so naturally that people never observe that you are doing it. But, if you are not smooth with them, every mistake and delay becomes a glaring error. Pretty soon, your timing and pacing have gone down the tubes and you are concentrating mostly on getting things going again. The cumulative effect is that people pay more attention to your miscues than they do to you or your visuals. Since most speakers don't use visuals all day every day, few can handle them smoothly. The only solution is to practice, practice, practice. Get so accustomed to using your visuals that you can do it in your sleep and even correct mistakes without a ripple. A good audio-visual presentation is like a dance routine. Timing and execution are everything. Remember, visuals are supposed to be aids, not stumbling blocks.

(11) *Plan for problems.* Murphy was right—at least when it comes to staging visual presentations. Something always seems to go wrong, no matter how much you've prepared. So, always have a solid Plan B. Build in good back up systems and maintain a good sense of humor. And, no matter how many times you've done it, or how familiar you are with the

systems, test everything one last time immediately before your presentation.

Visuals Are Worth The Risks

With all the problems and cautions I've cited, it might sound as if I'm negative on the idea of using visuals. Believe me, I'm not! I use a lot of visuals and highly recommend them. In our visual culture, they are becoming almost necessary.

My concern is that you control them like you control everything else in the speaking environment. That means they have to be carefully planned, thoroughly rehearsed and skillfully executed. If you are not willing to (or can't) invest the time needed to make them work right, you are better off without them.

If you use them artfully, they can be sheer dynamite. Here are only a few of the things they can do for you:

- Visuals can enliven a dull topic. Even volumes of figures and statistics can come alive with the use of pie and bar charts, and pictures can show how they relate to the real world.

- Visuals can boost your credibility. According to a study by 3-M Corporation, people view speakers who use overhead transparencies as more qualified and better prepared. Strong visuals add weight to everything you say.

- Visuals can enable you to cover more in less time. Your audience can grasp even the most complex ideas and information instantly with the aid of visuals.

- Visuals aid in retention. Studies show that people remember much longer, and in greater detail, what they see and hear than what they only hear.

In all, I think visuals are well worth the risks they entail. The secret is not to avoid, but to manage your risks.

Looking Ahead

Visuals are here to stay because they are so powerful and add so much energy to almost any presentation. In fact, with the rapid advances in technology, we may soon see a time when visuals will become as much a part of the speaking scene as lecterns have been in the past. It makes sense to learn how to use them well.

Perhaps the fastest growing and most commonly used form of audio-visual communication is television, in all its various forms. In our next chapter, let's see how you can get the most mileage out of this excellent communications vehicle.

CHAPTER TEN

COMING ACROSS ON VIDEO AND TV

"Video is a powerful communications tool . . . .
But no tool, however powerful it may be, can ever
replace the human element. The effectiveness of
the tool depends on the people using it."
—*Dubey and Bhanja*

Business leaders and professionals are beginning to pay more attention than ever to television as a viable means of reaching audiences that matter to them. And, more of them are finding that all it takes is a little preparation to be able to cash in on this powerful and all-pervasive medium.

- Donald Brown, M.D., one of San Francisco's leading cosmetic surgeons, discovered that local television news and talk shows provide an excellent means of gaining public recognition, without appearing to promote.

- Cheryl Stern, vice president and co-owner of a retail chain called The Gamekeepers, discovered that even a quickie on-the-spot news interview can be a boon to business, and that it's easier to handle than she thought.

- Philip E. Rollhaus, CEO of a large Chicago-based holding company called Quixote, Inc., discovered that videotapes provide an open and direct channel he can use to communicate with his executives, employees and even customers in remote locations, and who predicts that more and more executives will be using the medium in the coming years.

These represent only a small sampling of the many graduates of the ESE course who discovered the tremendous benefits of knowing how to work before video cameras.

In this chapter, I want to share with you some insights on how you can take some of the fear out of working with video and how you can look like a real pro every time you appear on television. Our focus here will be more on the technical aspects of working with cameras. In our next chapter, we'll look at the special techniques required to handle media interviews and difficult questions.

Video and TV Require Special Techniques

All of the speaking techniques we've discussed apply to working with video cameras, but television is such a unique medium that it requires its own special set of strategies and tactics.

Consider some of the special challenges video and TV offer:

(1) *The video camera is deadly in its accuracy and sensitivity to details*. It takes no prisoners. With strong lighting, powerful lenses and constant tracking, it captures every detail. Facial expressions and gestures that you could easily get away with on stage can make you look terrible when the camera zooms in for a close-up shot.

(2) *Studio microphones amplify every flaw*. If you get a frog in your throat on stage, you can simply turn your head and clear your throat. But television microphones are designed to track you like a bloodhound and record every noise you make. Studio mikes pick up and magnify every trace of accent, every verbal miscue and every stumble or stutter.

(3) *The bright lights play tricks on you*. If you have a tendency to perspire, they make you sweat. And, with the camera right there to pick up every bead of sweat, you can

come out looking like you are frightened half to death. Also, the bright lights do things to colors, so they can make you look washed out or almost ghastly.

(4) *The impersonality and confusion of the studio is vastly different from a live and responsive audience.* A talk that appears lively and filled with energy on stage can easily look dead and lifeless on television. Cameras don't show any response, so you never know how you're coming across. Plus it feels a little awkward to be trying to project enthusiasm or feel a sense of control on the tenth take or while you're listening to camera operators talk about how long it is until their break.

(5) *The hectic pace of television eats up time like crazy.* Points you can spend five minutes or more making on stage have to be made in 30 seconds or less on television. And, when you run out of time, you get cut off.

(6) *Audiences expect network quality, regardless of your budget.* With the average American watching seven hours of television every day, audiences have become geared to network quality. Since they have no idea how the shows are produced, people expect you to look like a network news anchor, and all your supportive videos to look like professionally filmed news footage.

(7) *Audiences aren't as courteous or attentive to television presenters as they are to stage speakers.* If they get bored, they'll flip channels or turn off the video recorder. If they get distracted, they'll tune you out for a while, then come back.

Have I frightened you away? I hope not because video not only enables you to reach more people than any other medium, you can often reach more people in one local news interview than in a lifetime of speaking to large audiences, and it can actually be fun once you learn some basics and practice them a few times.

Besides, there may be a video camera in your future sooner and more often than you think. Why? Technology is revolutionizing communications in our world and television, in a wide variety of forms, is the rising star.

Most major corporations now have their own video recording studios, and many either have their own networks or are connected through for-hire networks. Smaller firms now consider VCR units and large screen monitors to be minimal equipment for conference or training rooms.

By the end of the next decade, industry analysts predict that special television hookups, video-conferences and videotapes will provide the fastest and cheapest means for top executives to reach their employees, stockholders, customers and other groups.

Even if you're not yet paying attention to video, you can bet that your competitors are. Camera presence may very well be as critical to success in business as computer literacy is now.

How To Survive And Thrive
In The TV/Video Environment

Let's look at some simple techniques you can use to look and sound great on television. These work well in any form of video work, whether you are working live or videotaping an interview or presentation.

Technique #1:
Dress For The Camera

Generally, clothing that is suitable for business wear is also suitable for television. There are, however, some exceptions. Here is a list of do's and don't's about clothing for camera work.

DO:

- Wear mid-tone, soft and warm colors: Subdued shades of blue, gray, brown, green, lavender or burgundy are all good colors for suits, ties, scarves and dresses; pastels are good for shirts and blouses.

- Wear solid colors or very muted patterns.

- If you are seated: Men—unbutton your coat and pull it together in the front, straighten the bottom, tie your tie shorter than normal so it won't hang down between your legs, wear over-the-calf socks. Women—make sure your skirt covers your knees.

- Wear light-weight fabrics (even in the winter) that keep you cool under the bright lights.

DON'T:

- Wear whites, yellows, reds or drab grays.

- Wear bold patterns like plaids, stripes, polka dots, checks, herringbones or houndstooths.

- Wear vests or other tight-fitting clothes that can cut off circulation and make you look squeezed.

- Dress too casually or faddishly.

These guidelines are simple enough but they are extremely important. If you violate them, the camera can do funny things with your complexion or cause undesirable special effects.

Technique #2:
Use Makeup

The camera automatically seeks to balance all the shades, hues and intensities of color and lighting on the set. That means your face may look washed out, lines may be emphasized and dark spots under your eyes exaggerated.

Don't count on studio people to make you up; most of them get paid by the hour and may tell you that you look fine without makeup. So do your own make-up.

For women, it's mainly a matter of putting on more foundation and highlighters than for street wear. Use less eye shadow than normal.

Men can buy pancake makeup, to enrich their natural skin tones, and apply it in the restroom before they go on the set. The important thing is not to use plenty of it, but to cover all visible parts of your skin. If you have thin or light-colored eyebrows and lashes, you might want to wear mascara. If you are balding, a little powder on the head can soften the glare.

If you have the opportunity, experiment beforehand with similar lighting and cameras. In any case, ask for a videotape copy and assess how good your makeup looks before your next appearance.

Technique #3:
Control Your Expressions And Movements

Much of the time you're on camera, all the audience will see is your face, so your expressions and movements are greatly emphasized. For example, a slight frown can look like a nasty scowl and a slight twitch can look like a spastic jerk.

Try to look pleasant at all times, even when you are talking about a serious subject. Do let your face convey strong emotions and sincerity, and smile at every opportunity, but avoid wrinkling your forehead (when you are thinking or listening intently), and never tighten up your eyebrows.

You never can tell when the camera is in close, so you need to carefully control your movements at all times. Always keep your chin up and minimize the movements of your head. If you nod your head, do it ever so slightly and avoid making any major shifts with your body.

Don't fidget with your clothes or touch your face during filming, even if you think the camera is not on you. If you start sweating, ask to be "mopped" during a break.

Technique #4:
Use Your Gestures To Good Advantage

Gestures can enliven your appearance on a television camera. In fact, if you are good at using them, a director may pull the cameras back a little and show more long shots That can let you off the hook on so many close-ups.

But, when it comes to gestures on camera, a little goes a long way. Use tight, controlled gestures and make them fit precisely what you are saying at the time.

Keep your hands above your waist any time you want to make a special gesture. Actually, shoulder height is better. However, you have to be careful that you don't let your hands come between your face and the camera.

The use of gestures is one of those areas where a little practice can pay rich dividends.

Technique #5:
Exude Energy And Enthusiasm

It may seem like an impossible mission, with all that's going on around you, but high energy can do wonders to make you more interesting to watch.

You don't have to emote like a ham actor or try to come across like a television evangelist. Just show your excitement and conviction for what you are saying.

The two best places to let your energy and enthusiasm show are in your face and your voice. Raise your eyebrows, let the intensity show in your eyes and slightly exaggerate all your normal expressions. Put a lot of warmth and conviction in the tone of your voice and vary your volume to emphasize certain points.

Most of all, try to be warm, friendly and sincere. Let your viewers know you care.

Technique #6:
Look Into The Camera

Consider the camera your audience of one person and maintain flawless eye contact with it. Nothing destroys your credibility on television like failing to look into the camera.

If you have more than one camera, and you often will, always look at the one with the red light on. That will be the active camera.

When you are being interviewed by a host or there are other guests on the set and someone asks you a question, glance briefly at the person, then look right back into the camera. Remember, you are talking to the people on the other side of the television set, not to those in the studio.

And, never assume that the camera and microphone are turned off, even if someone signals "cut." It can be embarrassing to get caught giving a sigh of relief or making some dumb comment. Keep looking at the camera until some studio person steps on the set or until your host stands up.

Technique #7:
Compact And Enliven Everything You Say

On tape, every word, noise and grunt comes through. What sounds like interesting banter in private conversation sounds like endless rambling and stumbling around on video.

Therefore, it is vital to make every word and sound pay off. One of the best ways to counter the tendency to ramble is to know precisely what you are going to say and how you are going to say it. That's not always easy to do, especially when you are dependent on an interviewer's questions to guide your remarks. But, as you'll see in the next chapter, you can do a great deal to prepare for any kind of questions.

Practicing on audio tape is another good way to prepare. Practice saying things concisely. Practice getting to the point quickly and directly. Practice making every word count. Practice using short, crisp sentences.

Once you are on the set, speak distinctly and enunciate clearly, avoid stalling tactics like "uh," or "er," or "you know," and put all the warmth and energy you can into your voice.

Make your comments come alive by using active verbs and descriptive nouns and staying away from adjectives and adverbs. Give a complete response to any question you are asked and always avoid the temptation to answer with a simple "yes" or "no," or by merely nodding your head. You are there to express your views and ideas, not just give straight answers.

The greatest challenge can sometimes be to keep the flow moving. The one cardinal sin in any broadcast medium is excessive dead time—having nothing but silence on the air for 10 seconds or more. Respond quickly when someone throws the conversation your way and never pause more than five seconds in mid sentence. If you do, the host will probably jump in and interrupt you, just to get the show moving again.

You don't need to worry about the microphone. Once it has been strapped around your neck and you've given a sound level, it's up to the engineer to make sure you are heard clearly. Some studios will use a boom mike. Don't worry about it or keep looking up at it. Studio personnel are usually pretty good at having it at the right place at the right time, and boom mikes are too expensive to be dropped on the heads of guests.

Just concentrate on what you are saying and keep plenty of energy and conviction in your voice.

Special Strategies For Videotaped Presentations

More and more, executives and professionals are finding it advantageous to send out messages over closed-circuit networks, or pre-recorded videotapes or videodisks.

For example, the board chairmen of all three of the big three auto makers recently took to closed-circuit networks to announce their latest employee profit-sharing payouts. Like executives from most other major companies, they appear regularly on video to speak to employees, key managers, stockholders and even customers. It's a good way for a busy executive to add the personal touch in far-flung organizations.

But, as my friend and coaching client Philip Rollhaus discovered, making a professional-grade video can be an expensive and time-consuming challenge. He spent a day with me finding ways to improve the quality of his delivery and to reduce the enormously expensive time he had been spending on taping, retaping and editing.

Here are some of the strategies for videotaping presentations that he and I worked on, along with some ideas I've used with other professionals. These, of course, are in addition to all the ideas we've already covered.

Strategy #1:
Work From A Prepared Script

Earlier in the book, I recommended that you not read a speech, but videotaping is a special circumstance. It's the one place I highly recommend working from a prepared text.

The reason is that a video presentation has to be twice as smooth as a live presentation to look half as good. Besides, the expectations of your audience are based on the delivery and skill-level of the professionals they've seen on the major networks, and they all work from scripts. Subconsciously, your audience will be judging your message, delivery and credibility against network standards. It may be unfair, but that's the way it is in the real world. So you need to be GOOD!

Your script needs to be very tightly written and flow smoothly. I would suggest you get some professional help in the actual writing of it. You might want to prepare a rough draft, then call in a professional writer to tighten it up and smooth it out.

Once you get it back, go over it and read it aloud (preferably before a small video camera) to make sure you can say each word and phrase comfortably and that there are no tongue twisters you'll have to stumble through.

Another thing you need to do is cut it to the bone. Take out all superfluous words, change all passive verbs to active words and replace all weak words with strong ones.

Strategy #2:
Use A Teleprompter

A teleprompter is a device which displays your printed text on a screen beside the camera lens. If you read from the teleprompter, it creates the impression that you are looking directly into the camera.

The sheets of the text are strung together, so you don't have to turn pages. As you read along, an operator moves the text scroll up (on a "crawl") so that the line you are reading from is always near the center of the screen.

You can prepare your final text in ways that make it much easier for you to read. There are a number of ways to do this, and the trick is to find the one that works best for you.

One idea is to type all letters as capitals, because they are easier to read. Another is to use a punctuation mark at each logical pause, then to allow one extra white space between all in-sentence punctuation and two extra spaces between sentences. That way, you can easily see where the breaks are.

The formatting should also be easy to follow. You might start each new sentence (remember to use short sentences) at the beginning of a line, or you might want to leave an extra space between paragraphs.

Dr. Peter Marshall, who was the chaplain of the U.S. Senate for many years, developed a format for typing out his sermons that many speakers find to be perfect for use on a teleprompter. Here's a sample:

Dr. Marshall would start each new sentence flush left,
    each additional line would begin one tab space in,
    accenting the logical breaks,
    and so on.
When he started a new sentence,
    he would go back
    and pick up the same pattern.
That way, his eyes could easily find
    the beginning of his next sentence.
This format forced him to keep his sentences short,
    and eliminated the need for paragraphs.

The important thing is to find and use whatever layout is easiest for *you* to read. You need all the help you can get in achieving smoothness.

Strategy #3:
Practice, Practice, Practice

Practice, from the very beginning, reading with full expression and high energy. If possible, practice with a teleprompter at least several times before you go in to tape. The more natural it sounds to you, the easier it will be for your audience to follow and the more convincing you will be.

Remember to shoot for a conversational tone in your voice, not the typical reading tone. If you read it through enough times, you can almost speak it with only an occasional glance at the text.

As you practice reading through your script, look for good places to use pauses for emphasis. These pauses should last for about three to four seconds. That may seem a little long to you, but it will certainly add impact to your presentation.

Winston Churchill often used this technique in his speeches on radio, and the Britons would reportedly always sit up and lean toward the "wireless" to hear what was coming next. Of course, Sir Winston claimed that the reason for the pauses was so he could think up what to say next. But, since he always spoke from a prepared text, I think the old boy was putting us on.

The key to making pauses work on video is to look directly into the camera lens during each pause. Your audience will know that you are doing it intentionally and catch your emphasis.

One other helpful point about rehearsing is to practice reading a little faster than you normally talk. Slow talk on video sounds halting and tentative. It is almost impossible for most people to talk too fast for video, provided that they enunciate all words clearly.

Strategy #4:
Build In Cues

Write or draw in cues to remind yourself of special things you need to do to add more life to your presentation. These include things like smiling, raising your eyebrows, deepening your voice for effect, etc. All those things make you look more real and add variety to your delivery.

You can use verbal cues, if they work best for you. One famous orator used to write at various points in the margin of his speeches, "Shout loudly: weak point!"

Some speakers find it easier to use simple symbols which they devise for themselves. Some samples are:

A slash (/) = Pause.

Three slashes (/ / /) = Long pause.

Underline (_____) = Verbal emphasis.

Double underline (=====) = Strong emphasis.

Asterisk (*) = Smile.

Whatever system works best for you, giving yourself cues can help you to remember to add variety to your delivery. That can be a big help when you are taping in a studio where the peripheral activity resembles Grand Central Station.

Strategy #5:
Talk To One Person

Once the taping begins, try to visualize yourself talking to one person, a stranger, as if in an important and lively conversation. Imagine that you are telling that stranger something that you feel very strongly about and that the person is responding very positively to every word you are saying.

By doing this, you will be able to maintain a much more conversational tone to your voice, which is very important for video. An oratorical tone and manner will make you come across like a politician or a televangelist, and (after Richard Nixon, Gary Hart, Jim Bakker and Jimmy Swaggart) that's not the best company for a credibility-seeking professional to be in.

The reason it's important to think of the person as a stranger is that you might tend to be a little less energetic and enthusiastic with a friend. Notice sometime how people use a different tone and voice quality when they are talking to a stranger on a phone. It's a little more formal, a little more upbeat, there's more of a tendency to impress.

Video is a very personal and involving medium and it requires a highly personal touch. On the other hand, it's a medium that can make you look dead very easily, so it requires a great deal of energy. The balance between talking to one person, but thinking of that person as a stranger you want to impress, gives you the right mixture of credibility and energy.

Strategy #6:
Use A Natural Setting

If you have the option, always aim for a more natural setting than a lectern. Although most of the shots will be close enough that it won't show, it creates a barrier that can rob you of the advantage of intimacy with your audience.

Now, that brings up the question of what kind of setting. You could use a desk, but that seems a little stilted, too.

Some professionals try to get around the stilting problem by sitting on the front of their desks. That's hard to make look natural because most executives don't sit on the corner of their desks. So, it's a rather unnatural pose. Besides, most desk settings have rather bland colors for television.

One good option is a room setting with a sectional sofa. It can be colorful and it creates the feeling that a member of your audience could easily be sitting down with you for a chat. There is one caution: don't sit so far back in a huge plush sofa that it looks like it's swallowing you. Sit on the edge as if you are leaning forward because you are vitally interested in the conversation.

Another possible option is a setting on location. This means taking the camera out into a plant, a showroom, or some other setting that looks like a natural habitat for someone like you. Location shooting has the disadvantage of extraneous noise and poor recording acoustics. But it has so many advantages that it is often worth the sacrifice in sound quality. The two greatest advantages are that it greatly boosts your credibility and that it makes for very interesting and comfortable viewing by the audience.

There are some excellent combinations of studio-location taping, which brings up the next strategy.

Strategy #7:
Provide Visual Interest

Remember that people are accustomed to watching broadcast television, where action is the norm. To simply stand and talk for more than a couple of minutes can make viewers subconsciously start expecting a commercial break, and tune you out.

There are many ways to get around that problem. One is to tape part of the program in the studio and other parts of it at various locations. This works very well, if you do it right. If you choose this option, make sure that you use transitional statements to explain why you are jumping around and always give a reason for being in each location.

Another good option is to have a camera crew shoot some shots (they call it "wild footage") to splice in during the editing process. They simply take pictures on various locations, then electronically edit you out and the pictures in at designated points in the tape. It's the tactic used on network and local news all the time. This provides for a lot of visual interest and (since it can all be done by technical people) it speeds up the process considerably for you.

A rather expensive, but highly effective, combination of the two ideas I've just given you is to use a "chroma-key" system to electronically put you on location. What the technical people do is to tape the wild footage, then superimpose you over the pictures. This requires special equipment and taping techniques and must be planned for from the earliest stages. But it can make for a dynamite presentation.

Titles can also be used to provide visual interest. These can either be made from slides or you can get special effects and titles from computer genographics. The latter works better, but can be more expensive and may take longer to produce.

Looking Ahead

Video is an exciting and powerful way to communicate, if you know what you are doing. Hopefully, the techniques and strategies I've shared with you in this chapter will take some of the mystery out of it.

This is one of those areas where I highly recommend that you get some private coaching, especially if you plan to do a lot of video. There are so many personal issues that have to be dealt with, and the returns are so valuable, that the benefits far outweigh the investment.

Probably the most common exposure most executives and professionals have to video is being interviewed on talk shows or news programs. Such interviews can be frightening. In our last chapter, we'll zero in on how to handle the tough questions an interviewer, or anyone, might ask.

CHAPTER ELEVEN

HOW TO HANDLE TOUGH QUESTIONS

"The interviewer must be curious about *everything*."
—*Larry King*, Talk Show Host

Do you know what stress is? It's when your secretary interrupts a critical staff meeting and says, "Mike Wallace and a camera crew from *60 Minutes* are waiting for you in the lobby . . . . What shall I tell him?"

Not all questioners are as tough to handle as a muckraking media interrogator, and most business-related interviews are a piece of cake. But, occasionally, almost any business or professional leader gets caught in a web of tricky questions.

So, following the ancient wisdom that "a stitch in time saves nine," let's explore some effective strategies and tactics for handling tough questions, whether they come from an audience, the media, or some other source.

What Is A Tough Question?

To a high school student, a tough question is "One I don't know the answer to." Astute experts handle those questions with ease. They simply say, "I don't know, but I'll try to find out," or they can do the more common thing—shoot the bull.

What I call a tough question is one that can create or exacerbate a problem, almost any way you answer it, even if you refuse to answer it.

A problem may be anything from offending a group of

people who are important to your success to driving yourself out of business.

There are three important strategies for handling such questions:

(1) Recognize the questions and identify the risks.

(2) Anticipate the questions and prepare to answer.

(3) Turn the question into an opportunity.

We'll take a closer look at each of those strategies and some tactics for implementing them.

But first, let me avoid some trouble for myself. In certain circumstances, there may be legal consequences involved in answering questions. This chapter is designed to give general guidelines that apply to most situations—not as legal counsel for specific situations or actions. If there is any question in your mind about how to handle a specific question, I would suggest you seek the guidance of a competent attorney.

Strategy #1:
Recognize The Question And Identify The Risks

Oddly enough, the most common problem in handling questions is that business leaders fail to recognize how troublesome a question might be and don't weigh the risks it might involve.

Sure, anybody can spot trouble when a question is asked in a blatant way, like: "Senator, when did you quit beating your wife?"

But what if a reporter calls up and says, "I'm doing a survey of area businesses . . . . What is your policy about drugs in the workplace?" It may be a perfectly harmless question and one you'd gladly answer. Suppose, though, that the reporter has been talking to some of your disgruntled ex-employees, and the survey is just a ruse to trap you into a media confrontation with them. If so, almost any answer you give could lead to trouble.

It happens! Face the fact that almost any question, from any source, can be troublesome, whether the questioner intends it to be or not.

Media questions always bear watching. Why? It's a bottom-line fact of life. Bad news sells, good news doesn't sell. Newspapers, magazines and television and radio stations survive and thrive off bad news stories. Reporters and interviewers who find dirt and stir up controversy make more money and advance faster than those who don't. And, the more loudly you protest about their tactics, after the fact, the more additional money they make.

So, what do you do? Just take a "no comment" stance? That's usually worse. Depending on the question, a "no comment" can be interpreted as: "I'm guilty," or "We've got something to hide," or "I don't care," or "Let's fight." In the right circumstances, any one of those interpretations could lead to more trouble than an army of public relations people could handle.

I suggest you learn to recognize the types of questions that could be troublesome and to identify the risks they entail.

Types Of Troublesome Questions

Any question is potentially troublesome if you don't know what's behind it or fail to recognize its risks. There are, however, certain questions that by their very nature cry out for caution. Here are seven types of questions that should alert you to watch your step in answering.

(1) *The fishing expedition.* "I understand you are involved in merger talks with XYZ Company . . . . Is that correct?" The reporter may have no facts that would support a story and is hoping you will fill in the details. Always find out what the questioner already knows before commenting further.

(2) *Erroneous facts*. "So you have been charged by the FBI with interstate fraud?" Maybe some disgruntled customer in another state has accused you of fraud and threatened to go to the FBI. You need to find out if it's an honest mistake by the questioner or the false fact is used intentionally. If it's not intentional, you may be able to get by with simply supplying the correct information. But, if the questioner is out for blood, you need to watch every word you say.

(3) *The barb*. "How can you get away with ripping off your clients like that?" The question contains an accusation which is intended to get you rattled, in the hope that you'll make a fool of yourself. Keep your cool and talk positively about the value you offer your clients.

(4) *Misinterpreted statements*. "So your firm does discriminate against minorities, doesn't it?" What you said may have been, "No, we don't have an affirmative action hiring program in place at this time." The questioner is trying to put words into your mouth. You need to calmly correct the misinterpreted statement and make a positive statement of your own.

(5) *The setup*. Watch out any time a reporter or interviewer asks you a series of questions that require only a "yes" of "no" answer. The next one might be a real stinger. Most professional interviewers try to get you to talk as much as possible, not give a one word answer. If one deviates from that pattern, stay alert for the zinger and handle it carefully.

(6) *Hypothetical question*. "If the zoning commission does rule against your request, will you appeal the ruling in court?" Responding to "what if" questions can tip your hand on your next move, create adversary relationships, lock you into undesirable courses of action and cause many other problems. Avoid answering questions about what might happen and talk positively about what you are doing to head off any impending dangers.

(7) *Mud slinging invitation*. "Why do you think ABC Company (a competitor) is being investigated?" You may know exactly why and think they deserve it, but you'd better be careful about saying it. One thing to always keep in mind is that everybody usually gets dirty in a mud slinging contest— except the media, and they get rich.

How To Weigh The Risks Involved

Weighing the risks involved in answering a question, whether it comes from the media or a member of an audience calls for learning to think on your feet.

Teaching someone to do it is about as hard as trying to teach "court sense" in tennis or "savvy" in running a business. But there are a few tactics that do seem to help people develop those abilities.

The first one is to cultivate a certain mindset—a way of thinking things through to their next logical step. Learn to look for problems your answers might create. Ask, "How might someone interpret this statement negatively?" Read books and articles about handling media questions.

Second, observe how skilled interviewers get people to reveal information they'd just as soon not reveal, and how well-coached interviewees handle probing questions. I was fascinated, during the U.S. Senate subcommittee hearings on the Iran-Contra scandal, by the way certain senators asked questions to try to trap Colonel Oliver North into telling all and how he was able to turn every question into a favorable media event.

"You can see a lot if you just keep your eyes open," said that wise old sage of baseball, Yogi Berra.

The third way to improve your ability to think on your feet is to practice answering tough questions. Get an astute person (a staff member, a consultant, etc.) to play devil's advocate and throw tough questions at you. Record your answers, then analyze them to see how well you handled the task. The more you practice in a safe setting, the better equipped you'll be to deal with the real world.

Strategy #2:
Anticipate And Prepare For Troublesome Questions

Astute business leaders go looking for trouble before it comes looking for them. They take a proactive stance on questions they might be asked.

Here are some tactics that can help you do that.

(1) *Start by identifying the public relations risks involved in your industry or profession and in your own business operation.*

Look at all the areas of your business that could cause the media or members of an audience to ask questions that could put you on the defensive.

If, for example, you are in an industry that has to dispose of hazardous waste, that's a ticking time bomb. Anything that has to do with the environment can create problems with various public interest groups, employees and even your customers.

There are many areas all businesses need to be concerned about: employment practices, safety issues, liability issues, community responsibility, etc.

Any time you see a professional or a company under fire in the media, ask if that is a potentially explosive area for you.

It might even be worthwhile to call in a public relations firm to make recommendations as to what bases you need to cover and how to go about it.

Identifying potential problems is a little like deciding what kind of insurance you need to buy, except it's much cheaper.

(2) *Make a list of the 10 toughest questions you could be asked and pre-determine how you would answer them.* This is a good tactic whether you are going for an interview,

preparing to answer questions after a speech, or if you simply want to be ready when the time comes.

Call in your key people, and anyone else who can help you, and brainstorm all the negative questions people could ask, however farfetched those questions may seem. Then, prepare the most constructive answer you can give for each.

If this seems like a pessimistic approach to you, consider this: salespeople do it all the time. They call it anticipating objections. It's simply a matter of predicting what negative responses they might get and thinking through the best ways to handle them.

One benefit to anticipating the hard questions is that, if you do a thorough job of it, you won't have to do it again. You can just keep the questions and answers on file and review them periodically. It may also be a good idea to make sure all the key people in your organization are familiar with those questions and answers.

(3) *Consider ways you might head off troublesome questions.* There is often a big difference between the perceptions of the public or a group and the realities of your operation. Sometimes, troublesome questions are totally unjustified, but that doesn't mean they will never be asked.

You can often head off problematic questions and charges by taking proactive measures. The major oil companies, for example, invested millions of dollars in advertising to make the public aware of all they are doing to protect the environment. Positive media campaigns work.

Another approach is to collect solid data, perhaps even do some basic research, to support your position on troublesome issues. Keep that data on file and updated, just in case you need it. Often, the best answer to a troublesome question or charge is hard evidence that negates it.

(4) *Prepare a damage containment plan in advance.* When the makers of Tylenol were hit by the cases of arsenic poisoning a few years ago, they had a damage containment plan

in place and were able to respond very quickly and protect themselves from total disaster.

Within hours, the president of the company was on the air expressing concern for the well-being of the victims and assuring the public that they were as alarmed as anyone about the problem. He outlined strong steps that were being taken, including taking the product off the market until the source of the arsenic could be found. He went on to ask for any ideas as to how they could do more.

The net result was that public confidence in the company went up, not down.

What would you do if a public relations disaster hit your company? It's best to know in advance.

Strategy #3:
Turn Questions Into Opportunities

The Napa Valley Vintner's Association asked my firm to conduct a series of workshops with their members to prepare for the annual barrage of questions from reporters and the hundreds of thousands of visitors who pour into the valley for their much celebrated wine tastings.

Usually these events are totally positive and they are a great boon to the vintners. Yet, most guides and executives who've been at it a while have experienced the tough questions that always seem to come up, sometimes in the worst ways and at the worst times.

"How can you justify contributing to the massive problem of alcoholism in this country?" someone always asks. Others will ask vintners about individual concerns: "Why is your wine so expensive (or cheap)?" or "Why don't your labels list the pesticides you use?"

The association knew that a few explosive answers from individuals could create a major controversy that would overshadow the positive effects of the event and the many valuable contributions of the whole industry.

One of the strategies we taught spokesmen from more

than 100 wineries was turning negative questions into positive opportunities. Let me share with you some of the tactics we taught them to use.

(1) *Don't let them see you squirm.* No matter how rattled or angry you may feel inside, it won't help your cause to let your questioner or anyone else know it. If you are dealing with a skilled interviewer or a potentially hostile audience, the sight of blood will only egg them on.

You don't need to lie and say, "I'm glad you asked that question." But you do need to stay calm and positive in your response.

Whatever you do, don't attack your questioner personally or hit out at the institution he or she represents. Stick to the issue.

This is why advance preparation and practice are so valuable. If you've answered similar questions in rehearsals, and have prepared yourself emotionally, you won't be caught off guard when it happens in real life.

You may even be able to laugh it off, which is a good ploy.

(2) *Defuse the question.* Sometimes, you can blunt the question by taking the sting out of it with humor.

First Lady-to-be Barbara Bush gave one of the best demonstrations of this tactic I've ever seen, in a TV interview during the 1988 presidential campaign. Host Kathleen Sullivan was sailing along with soft questions and suddenly threw in a bomb. "Would you borrow a dress?" It was obvious that she was trying to trap Barbara into either defending or attacking Nancy Reagan for borrowing dresses from designers, a subject the media had been having a field day with. Barbara, who was a little hefty, took all the sting out of the question by smiling broadly, gesturing to emphasize her size and asking her host: "Really, Kathleen, how easy do you think it would be for me to borrow a dress?" Kathleen gulped, then went right on to another line of questioning. Barbara Bush had made her look like an ogre without even putting her down.

A softening statement can often defuse a sharp question. I suggested that the vintners defuse the alcoholism question with a statement like: "We share your concern about alcoholism. . . we feel it is a serious problem in this country . . . ."

Sometimes, a simple acknowledgement that it's a valid question can take some of the sting out of it, and give you some time to think. "That's a fair question, and I'll try my best to answer it as honestly as I can . . . ."

(3) *Get off the defense.* I'm an avid tennis buff, and I learned early on that the best you can hope to do on defense is to keep your opponent from scoring. You can only score when you're on the offense. It's the same way with troublesome questions. Somehow you have to seize the initiative.

One way to do that is to offer a softening statement, then go right into a series of positive statements. "We share your concern about alcoholism . . . we feel it is a serious problem in this country . . . . That's why we promote wine as a food."

Another way to seize the initiative is to challenge the premise of the question. "For me to answer that question would be to assume that our client is guilty, and we believe that in this country a person is innocent until proven guilty."

Your objective is always to move quickly from defending your position to scoring positive points.

(4) *Make them come after you.* If you sense that the questioner is out for blood, or don't understand what's behind it, sometimes the best thing to do is run and make the person come after you.

You can do this by asking your own question: "You must have a reason for asking that question . . . . Do you mind if I ask what it is?" If there is a hidden agenda, this will usually smoke it out.

Or, you might just plead ignorance: "I don't understand!" You don't have to explain what you don't understand; just make the statement and wait. The next move is up to the questioner.

You might even appeal to the human kindness of the questioner, or the audience: "Wow! I could get fired for answering that question."

What's important in using this tactic is to throw the ball back into the other court and force the questioner to mount a full scale attack.

Of course, you have to be careful not to yield the floor for someone to make a long negative speech, so you have to use this one carefully.

(5) *Buy some time, if you need it.* There may be a legitimate reason that you cannot answer a question at the moment. If so, buy some time until you can answer it safely.

A good way to do that is to be completely open and above board: "I hope you can understand that it would be very unwise for me to say anything on that subject until . . . . When that happens, I'll be glad to cooperate fully. You have my word on it . . . . Thank you for respecting my position on this."

That's a nice way to say "no comment," without sounding like you've got something to hide.

(6) *Sometimes, the best defense is a good offense.* One of the best ways to deal with troublesome questions is to head them off before they come up.

Let's say, for example, you are going to be interviewed by a reporter or talk show host, on a variety of subjects.

Usually, all a reporter is looking for is an interesting story, or a few good quotes to embellish a larger story. They are trained to keep digging until one is found. All most hosts want is a lively discussion on a vital topic.

So, why not give them what they want instead of waiting for them to come after it? Start out the interview with an important announcement, or suggest a direction for a good story, or start spouting out very quotable ideas.

If the questioner is on a fishing expedition, which is often the case, a big catch will divert attention away from an explosive issue which might come up in routine questioning.

The key to making this one work is to make sure there is a legitimate story (from the reporter's viewpoint) in what you are offering. Puff on company products or tooting your own horn won't get it.

Looking Ahead

Of course, none of these strategies and tactics works all the time and sometimes you'll have to use a combination of them. The important point is to realize that troublesome questions will come up from time to time and that it is vital to know in advance how you will handle them.

Now, it's time to explore briefly how you can most effectively use all the exciting things we've discovered together in this book.

AFTERWORD

The personal presence and power you develop as a result of utilizing the speaking techniques in this book can pay rich dividends in many ways, especially in your career.

George D. Ebersole, president of Chicago-based Energy Absorption Systems, Inc., once told me that he believed the ability to present ideas effectively is the most crucial factor in a person's professional life.

"I can usually judge how well people are going to do in our company just by watching how they respond to what they learn in the Executive Speaking Experience," George said. He and all his key people have gone through our program and constantly use the ideas and techniques they've learned to stimulate each other to keep growing and learning.

"If I see someone grasping your ideas and getting better and better at using them, I figure that person will make a valuable contribution to our efforts," he observed. "If not, I usually write them off as not being the kind of person we want to invest a lot of time and money in developing further."

I share this in closing to remind you that you never know who is watching or listening to you speak. Think about it. Does every presentation you give prove to all present that you are the kind of person who is worth developing further, or investing money with, or entrusting with important projects?

How Good Do You Want To Be?

My vintner friends tell me that wine must be aged before it can reach its full potential. But, before it can begin the crucial curing process, it must be properly prepared.

The same is true of speakers: they get better with experience. As Doctor Donald Brown says: "Speaking is like practicing medicine. You have to know a great deal about it before you can begin doing it, and you have to practice a great deal before you can become good at it."

Speaking is one of those things of which it can accurately be said; "It's easy if you work hard at it, but it can be extremely hard if you work easy at it."

One of my favorite stories is about a young man who once approached a great concert pianist and asked the secret of his enormous talent.

"Practice, my boy," said the maestro. Then, he went on to explain that he practiced eight hours every day.

"But, sir!" shouted the astonished young man, "You are so good! Why do you keep practicing so much every day?"

"Because," the old master replied with a twinkle in his eye, "I wish to be superb!"

That's my wish for you—that you will keep working at speaking, and keep practicing until you become superb. If you do that, you will find it easy, productive and fun.

SUGGESTED READING

Alessandra, Anthony J., Ph.D. and Phillip S. Wexler, *Non-Manipulative Selling* (Prentice Hall, Englewood Cliffs, NJ, 1987)

Ailes, Roger, *You Are The Message* (Doubleday, Homewood, Illinois, Dow Jones-Irwin, 1988).

Axtell, Roger E., *Do's and Taboos Around the World* (The Parker Pen Company, 1987)

Bayan, Richard, *Words that Sell* (Contemporary Books, Inc., Chicago, Illinois, 1987)

Bennis, Warren G., *Leaders: The Strategies of Taking Charge* (Harper & Row, NY, NY, 1986)

Covey, Stephen R., *The 7 Habits of Highly Effective People* (Simon & Schuster, NY, NY, 1989)

Dyer, Wayne W., *You'll See It When You Believe It* (Morrow, NY, NY, 1990)

Frank, Milo O., *How to Get Your Point Across in 30 Seconds or Less* (Simon & Schuster, NY, NY, 1987)

Garfield, Charles A., *Peak Performers* (Nightingale/Conant, 1988)

Hart, Lois B. and J. Gordon Schlelcher, *A Conference and Workshop Planner's Manual* (AMACOM, 1979)

Helmstetter, Shad, *The Self-Talk Solution* (Morrow, NY, NY, 1988)

Helmstetter, Shad, *What To Say When You Talk To Yourself* (Leadership Dynamics, 1986)

Kenny, Michael, *Presenting Yourself* (Eastman Kodak Company, 1982)

Linkletter, Art, *Public Speaking for Private People* (Bobbs-Merrill Company, 1980)

McManus, Ed and Bill Nicholas, *We're Roasting Harry Tuesday Night* (Prentice Hall, Englewood Cliffs, NJ, 1984)

Molloy, John T., *Molloy's Live For Success* (Perigord Press, 1985)

Murphy, Dr. Joseph, *The Power of Your Subconscious Mind* (Prentice Hll, Englewood Cliffs, NJ, 1989)

Nathan, Erenst D., *Twenty Questions on Conference Leadership* (Addison-Wesley Publishing Company, 1988)

Newman, Edwin, *Strictly Speaking* (Warner Books, NY, NY, 1988)

Orben, Bob, *2500 Jokes to Start 'em Laughing* (Coubleday & Company, 1980)

Vardaman, George T., *Making Successful Presentations* (AMACOM, 1984)

Williams, Judy, *How to Plan and Book Meetings and Seminars* (Ross Books, 1987)

Wilson, Larry, *Changing The Game* (Nightingale/Conant, 1988)

Ziglar, Zig, *See You At The Top* (Pelican, 1984)

INDEX

Countdown to a Powerful Presentation!
A New Audio Cassette Tape
Produced and narrated by Lynda R. Paulson
President, Success Strategies, Incorporated

- 7 Steps to a Dynamite Delivery
- Affirmations to Relieve Anxiety and Focus Energy
- 12 Checkpoints for Effective Preparation and Rehearsal

Lynda Paulson's compelling 45-minute audio cassette is your personal warm-up before every speech and presentation you give. Listen in your car, at home or at the office.

☐ **Yes,** I want positive audience response every time. Send me _____ copies of the 45-minute audio cassette:

Countdown To A Powerful Presentation

$9.95 plus $1.50 shipping & handling
Phone orders accepted (800) 776-1310 or (707) 255-1310

☐ Check enclosed   ☐ MasterCard   ☐ Visa

CARD NUMBER _____ EXP. _____

SIGNATURE _____

NAME _____

COMPANY _____

STREET ADDRESS _____

CITY _____ STATE _____ ZIP_____

Please photocopy or detach and mail to:

Success Strategies, Inc.
1325 Imola Avenue West
Suite 404
Napa, CA 94559

The Executive Speaking Experience

A Success Strategies, Inc. Seminar

A powerful, personal three-day program
for everyone who communicates for a living

The ESE Promise:
- Heightened confidence and ability to get your message across
- Competent, graceful management of your voice, body, movements, gestures, breathing and facial expressions
- Resolution of speaking-related anxiety
- Mastery at handling provocative and confrontational issues
- Savvy to handle media, props and visual aids
- New TV and video skills
- Higher level of comfort and control

What Makes This Course Exceptional?
- Fifteen times in front of the camera
- Smaller class size
- Personalized attention to each individual
- Private follow-up coaching

You can persuade, sell, motivate and inspire

References gladly offered   Results are fully guaranteed
Tailored in-house sessions and private coaching

Success Strategies, Inc.
**1325 Imola Avenue West
Suite 404
Napa, CA 94559
1-800-776-1310**

Who Needs a Copy of This Book?

☐ **Yes,** I would like to order:
The Executive Persuader: How To Be A Powerful Speaker
by Lynda R. Paulson

Please send me _____ copies at $19.95 $ _____

Shipping/handling ($3.50 per book) $ _____

($1.50 each additional book) $ _____

TOTAL $ _____

☐ Check enclosed   ☐ MasterCard   ☐ Visa

Card Number _____ Exp. _____

Signature _____

Phone orders accepted (800) 776-1310 or (707) 255-1310
(Volume discounts available. Please inquire.)

☐ Please send information about the *Executive Speaking Experience* seminar.
☐ Please send information about other Success Strategies seminars:
   ☐ **Teambuilding**
   ☐ **Retail Sales**
   ☐ **Customer Service**
   ☐ **Leadership**
   ☐ **Train the Trainer**

NAME _____

COMPANY _____

STREET ADDRESS _____

CITY _____ STATE _____ ZIP _____

Please photocopy or detach and mail to:

Success Strategies, Inc.
1325 Imola Avenue West
Suite 404
Napa, CA 94559
(800) 776-1310